DATE DUE		
MAR 2 '83	Aug 12 '94	
MAR 31 '84	AP 17 '96	
APR 28 '84	AG 11 '99	
DEC 7 '85		
AUG 25 '86		
SEP 30 '86		
APR 8 '91		
SEP 13 '91		
OCT 23 '91		
SEP 0 8 1992		
APR 2 2 1993		
JUL 2 9 1994		

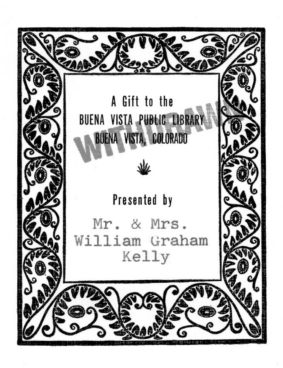

A Gift to the
BUENA VISTA PUBLIC LIBRARY
BUENA VISTA, COLORADO

Presented by

Mr. & Mrs.
William Graham
Kelly

CAVALRY LIFE

IN

TENT AND FIELD

MRS. ORSEMUS BRONSON BOYD
(Frances Anne Mullen Boyd)

INTRODUCTION BY
Darlis A. Miller

————

UNIVERSITY OF NEBRASKA PRESS
Lincoln AND *London*

Introduction copyright © 1982 by the University of Nebraska Press
Manufactured in the United States of America

First Bison Book printing: 1982
Most recent printing indicated by the first digit below:
1   2   3   4   5   6   7   8   9   10

Library of Congress Cataloging in Publication Data
Boyd, Orsemus Bronson, Mrs.
Cavalry life in tent and field.

Reprint. Originally published: New York : J. S. Tait, 1894. (Tait's Kenilworth series ; no. 5)
1. Boyd, Orsemus Bronson, Mrs. 2. West (U.S.)—Description and travel—1860–1880. 3. United States. Army—Military life. 4. West (U.S.)—Biography. 5. Army wives—West (U.S.)—Biography. I. Title.
II.   Series: Tait's Kenilworth series ; no. 5.
F594.B8 1982   978'.02'0924 [B]   81–19772
ISBN 0–8032–1176–7   AACR2
ISBN 0–8032–6063–6 (pbk.)

REPRINTED FROM THE 1894 EDITION PUBLISHED BY J. SELWIN TAIT & SONS, NEW YORK

INTRODUCTION
by Darlis A. Miller

IN THE TWENTY-FIVE YEARS following the Civil War, as thousands of settlers were lured west by prospects of finding new homes, fertile fields, rich mineral veins, and a fresh start, no area of the western United States remained unaffected by the deadly struggle between emigrants and American Indians to control the land.

The primary responsibility for protecting settlers and pacifying the tribes fell to the frontier army, whose strength during most of these years was limited by law to 25,000 officers and enlisted men, a force always too small to cope adequately with angry Indians. Scattered in tiny contingents among some two hundred isolated posts, the enlisted men and officers lived in a closely regulated military society and experienced a way of life unlike that of most settlers. A few women—laundresses, servants, wives and daughters of officers and enlisted men— shared this strange and often dangerous existence.

Although their numbers were small, officers' wives assumed positions of prominence at the frontier posts, enjoying the respect of the entire garrison and making life for their husbands less onerous than it might otherwise have been. Many women recorded their army experiences in diaries, in long descriptive letters to friends back home, and in memoirs written after they returned east and made their final "severance" from the military. The women proved able observers. In their writings, they focused primarily on the domestic side of army life, documenting the difficulties and joys of raising families and making homes in primitive surroundings. They also recorded fascinating observations about frontier settlements, local inhabitants, military personnel, tribal customs, modes of transportation, and numerous other facets of western society.

Frances A. Boyd's *Cavalry Life in Tent and Field* (originally published in 1894) recounts her life as an officer's wife between 1867 and 1885, years which witnessed the final subjugation of most western tribes and their forced removal to reservations. The author followed her husband, Orsemus Bronson Boyd, from one military assignment to another, making a home for themselves and, eventually, their three children at frontier posts in Nevada, Arizona, New Mexico, and Texas. The book presents an intimate account of everyday life at several southwestern army garrisons. It also stands as a tribute to the author's husband, praising his courage and his devotion to country.

Orsemus B. Boyd, son of Henry and Eliza Bronson Boyd, was born in 1844 near Croton (now called Treadwell), New York. At the start of the Civil War, he enlisted in the New York Volunteers with his father and older brother, but he resigned in 1863 to accept appointment to West Point. The injustices he suffered during his cadet years are briefly described in the author's Preface. Boyd graduated from the academy in 1867 and was commissioned a second lieutenant in the Eighth Cavalry. He was promoted to first lieutenant in 1868 and remained in that rank fourteen years, receiving appointment as captain in 1882. After a brief illness while on campaign against Geronimo, Boyd died at a military camp near Grafton, New Mexico, on July 23, 1885, at the age of forty-one.

In her book, Frances Boyd says practically nothing about her own origins and writes of her husband's family rather than her own. She is reluctant to identify individuals, failing to give, for example, the first names either of herself (Frances or Fannie) or of her three children (Mabel, James, and Henry). She mentions having two brothers, one living in Chicago and the other in Cheyenne, Wyoming. One of the brothers later moved to Silver City, New Mexico, where he edited a newspaper. But she provides no further identification of these family members, even though the book is dedicated to a brother named James.[1] We do know, however, that she was born in New York City on February 14, 1848 and was christened Frances Anne Mullen. She spent most of her youth in New York City, where she married Orsemus Boyd on October 9, 1867.

Shortly after the wedding, Lieutenant Boyd was ordered to Camp Halleck, Nevada, where U.S. soldiers were protecting the surveying and construction crews of the Central Pacific Railroad. Frances Boyd followed her husband west in January 1868. This journey to Nevada must have been a stupendous adventure for the young bride: she boarded a steamer in New York, crossed Panama by train, journeyed by steamer to San Francisco and then to Sacramento, where she boarded a train to Cisco (then the terminus of the Pacific Railroad), crossed the Sierras by sled and stagecoach, and finally completed the trip to Camp Halleck in army ambulance and an open wagon.

The Boyds left Camp Halleck in January 1869 bound for San Francisco, where Frances gave birth to their first child, Mabel. Shortly thereafter, the family traveled by steamer to southern California and then overland by army wagon, first to Fort Mojave, Arizona, and then to Camp Date Creek, where Lieutenant Boyd served from May 1869 to March 1870. Arizona at this time was a sparsely settled territory, plagued by bitter Indian-white hostilities. Primitive living conditions, harsh climate, and the inhospitable desert made army life strenuous and difficult.

Boyd's regiment subsequently was ordered to Fort Stanton, New Mexico, where the lieutenant was stationed from April 1870 to October 1871. The post was located in pine-covered hills near Sierra Blanca, and Frances found the climate and countryside a bracing contrast to the desolate environment of Camp Date Creek. She left Fort Stanton, however, during the spring of 1871 to visit friends in New York and to await the arrival of their second child, James. Obtaining a leave of absence, Lieutenant Boyd joined his wife in the East shortly before their son's birth. By the summer of 1872, the Boyds had returned to New Mexico, residing first at Fort Union, a comfortable post about one hundred miles east of Santa Fe, and then at Fort Bayard, located in the remote southwestern corner of the territory among the rolling hills approaching the Santa Rita Mountains. They remained at Fort Bayard from March 1873 to December 1875.

Lieutenant Boyd and his regiment were then ordered to Fort Clark, Texas, an important post guarding the San Antonio–El Paso road, located forty miles from the Rio Grande and the Mexican border. The Boyds spent nearly five years in Texas, and their second son, Henry, was born there in 1877. For six months, spanning the winter of 1879/80, the family lived at Fort Duncan, Texas, located on the left bank of the Rio Grande at Eagle Pass, where troops patrolled the international boundary. When Mabel and James fell seriously ill with malaria in 1881, Frances Boyd returned to New York with the children. During the fall of that year, her husband requested and was appointed to recruiting service in the East, enabling the family to live together briefly at his new post in Boston.[2] Frances and the children returned to New York, however, when Orsemus was transferred to Davenport, Iowa, and the family remained separated while he later served at Rochester, New York, and at Jefferson Barracks, Missouri. Boyd subsequently returned to

Texas, followed during the spring of 1885 by his wife, daughter, and possibly one son. Four months after their arrival at Fort Clark, Captain Boyd was ordered to New Mexico to take part in the Apache campaign. His death in July left Frances Boyd bereft of husband and home. After nearly eighteen years of marriage to an officer, her ties with the army were abruptly severed.

Frances Boyd was a competent and entertaining writer—and, more than that, she was an observant woman with a great curiosity about the West and its people. She shared these characteristics with other women writers who married into the military, including Elizabeth B. Custer, whose *"Boots and Saddles," Tenting on the Plains,* and *Following the Guidon* appeared in print between 1885 and 1890; Lydia Spencer Lane, author of *I Married a Soldier,* published in 1893; and Martha Summerhayes, whose minor classic, *Vanished Arizona,* was published in 1908.

Most women who wrote about their army experiences had been raised in sheltered eastern households and were totally unprepared for life on the frontier. Frances Boyd admits that before her marriage she considered New York City "the only habitable place on the globe"[3] (*Cavalry Life,* p. 23). And she was not the only young army bride who traveled west dreaming that all military posts would resemble West Point. Inexperienced and ignorant about cooking and domestic chores, she must have found army life a rude shock.

With steadfast courage and abundant good humor, however, most young wives adjusted to frontier hardships and grew to love the service. It was a rigorous existence, but they embarked upon their new lives with a keen sense of adventure. Even at the most primitive military post, Frances Boyd willingly endured many hardships to share this life with her husband. While living in New York awaiting the birth of her second child, she grew homesick for the freedom and wild beauty of her western home.

And she undoubtedly agreed with Martha Summerhayes, who declared: "I had cast my lot with a soldier and where he was, was home to me."[3]

Army women were human, of course, and when occasion warranted they complained about the less attractive features of military life. Several had difficulty adjusting to the rudimentary housing found at army posts. General William T. Sherman thought it a crime that enlisted men were forced to live in damp, overcrowded, vermin-infested barracks—structures unfit, he said, even for horses. Officers' quarters frequently were no better; medical records described those at Camp Verde, Arizona, as "miserable hovels." Most officers' wives lived in tents during some portion of their military careers. Frances Boyd, arriving at Camp Halleck in a snowstorm, was dismayed to discover that her home consisted of two wall tents.

The women shared with soldiers the vicissitudes of weather. Summer temperatures in Arizona commonly reached as high as 100 to 120 degrees; winter temperatures on the Northern Plains dropped as low as 60 degrees below zero. These subzero temperatures could result in severe frostbite, and some soldiers died from exposure. The Boyds, while living under canvas at Camp Halleck, suffered both from winter cold (33 degrees below zero) and from summer heat (the sun penetrated the thin canvas, burning exposed skin.)

Army pay was hardly adequate. The army provided officers with quarters, fuel, and medical care, but rations, travel expenses, household furnishings, and other necessities came out of an officer's salary. A first lieutenant's pay of about $133 a month in greenbacks did not go very far on the frontier, where the cost of supplies was exorbitant and where merchants discounted paper money as much as 50 percent of its face value. Lydia Lane asserted that it was "almost impossible for an army officer to save money. His pay barely suffices for his monthly expenses, and he feels much gratified if after his bills are settled he has anything left over."[4]

Some supplies, such as fresh fruits, vegetables, eggs, and butter, were difficult to obtain at any price. Many officers and their families subsisted for months (the Boyds, for three years) on the same basic staples that the army fed to enlisted men: bacon, flour, beans, coffee, tea, rice, and sugar. When the commissary or post sutler was able to stock canned peaches and other delicacies, officers eagerly purchased them to supplement the family's diet. At many frontier posts, mountain trout, venison, buffalo meat, wild turkey, and other game furnished variety to the menu.

Among the greatest worries besetting army women were childbirth and rearing of children at frontier posts. Frequently an officer's wife was the only woman in the garrison. A new mother could feel very lonely—and she had no female help or companionship while giving birth or caring for the newborn infant. At larger posts, where there were more officers' wives, women provided mutual support and became competent midwives from necessity. Nevertheless, some army women, because of the hardships and discomforts of frontier life, tried to prevent unwanted pregnancies. Others experienced difficult or near-fatal complications at childbirth. Frances Boyd's complications after the birth of her first child resulted in part from her own inexperience and from the lack of a competent nurse to attend her. And despite Boyd's assertion that children thrived in western climates, infant mortality rates were high. Many army families, like their civilian counterparts, buried one or more children in isolated western cemeteries. Nineteenth-century medical knowledge was primitive, and army doctors often lost their battles against childhood diseases. Yet many officers' wives, including Frances Boyd, paid tribute in their memoirs to kindhearted army surgeons who ministered to their families.

Whenever possible, officers' wives employed servants or enlisted men to help with household chores and the care of children. This did not mean that army women were pampered; they
performed many time-consuming and back-breaking tasks, enduring all the inconveniences associated with the army's
peripatetic way of life. Rather, in relieving them from some of
the household drudgery, the employment of servants gave officers' wives time for other pursuits: self-improvement, tutoring
of children, nursing the sick, organizing entertainments for the
garrison.

Women and soldiers alike found camp life dull and monotonous. The boredom bred petty jealousies and contributed to a
high suicide rate among enlisted men. Soldiers preferred scout
and escort duties, and when they went on campaign, the garrison became even more lonely and monotonous for the women
left behind. Certainly the greatest fear most army women experienced occurred while the men were on campaign: they feared
for their husbands' safety. That suspense, Elizabeth Custer
declared, was "the hardest of all trials that come to the soldier's
wife."[5] Resources were limited for altering the stupefying
sameness of days spent in garrison. Army men therefore appreciated the entertainments that women devised to bring di-
versity to their lives. Frances Boyd mentions dances, masquerade and card parties, and amateur theatricals as favorite
forms of amusement. For personal diversion, she went fishing
and horseback riding, visited neighboring settlements, devoured books and magazines, and gossiped with other officers'
wives. A rigid military caste system, however, kept officers'
wives apart from laundresses and wives of enlisted men.

Although Boyd disliked the frequent moves and uncertainties
of army life, she grew to appreciate the variety that western
travel brought to her life. She encountered many Indians and
Hispanos and in her book she shows them in a positive light. She

describes with sympathy the friendly Piute and Shoshone Indians of Nevada and the Pimas and Maricopas of Arizona. She characterizes Hispanic families with whom she lodged as gentle people, "who in their simple kindness were most truly hospitable. They made us welcome, and yet exacted no reward for the time and attention bestowed" (pp. 172–73). Although biases are apparent in her writing (she perpetuates the image of the lethargic Mexican laborer, for example), Boyd is remarkably open-minded compared with other western travelers.

In time, she found much to admire in the western landscape. She became almost lyric in describing the countryside surrounding Fort Stanton: "The climate was perfect, the air so exquisitely pure as to lend a freshness and charm to each day's existence. To breathe was like drinking new wine" (p. 175). Even the limitless western prairies held special charm for Boyd. "In those grand wastes," she wrote, "one is truly alone with God" (p. 182). Although she viewed the West as a region awaiting economic development, she clearly rejoiced in having seen many of its grandeurs—including the White Sands of New Mexico—before later emigrants marred their beauty.

Boyd reserved her highest praise for the men and women of the frontier army. She endured many of the same hardships and privations they endured. She shared their danger while traveling through country claimed by unfriendly Indians. She saw middle-aged officers become old men because of the constant exposure to the elements. And she assisted in burying officers' wives whose health had been broken by their frontier experience. "Surely," she exclaimed, "in no other life can women be found who are at once so brave and true" (p. 228).

Frances Boyd obviously found happiness in the western army, and she tells her story with spirit and considerable humor. The reception that her book received in military circles upon publication is not known, but it hardly made a ripple on the world's literary scene. It received modest attention in the *Dial*, whose reviewer described the book as readable and informative. The *New York Times* reviewer was less kind, criticizing the author for showing dissatisfaction with certain aspects of military life and implying that women had no place in the frontier army. Present-day researchers are more appreciative of the book's merits. They frequently quote from it in articles and books about western women and the frontier army.

Frances Boyd died on May 2, 1926, at the age of seventy-eight, having lived the last years of her life on her estate, "Alancourt," in Boonton, New Jersey. She never received in her lifetime the praise that readers now accord her military memoir.

NOTES

1. James Mullen edited at least two Silver City newspapers between 1877 and 1883.

2. Frances Boyd used few dates in her memoir, and she erred in stating that her husband received recruiting duty in 1882. Military records show he was assigned this duty in 1881.

3. Martha Summerhayes, *Vanished Arizona: Recollections of the Army Life of a New England Woman* (Lincoln: University of Nebraska Press, 1979), p. 204.

4. Lydia Spencer Lane, *I Married a Soldier; or, Old Days in the Old Army* (Albuquerque: Horn and Wallace, 1964), p. 152.

5. Elizabeth B. Custer, *"Boots and Saddles"; or, Life in Dakota with General Custer* (Norman: University of Oklahoma Press, 1961), p. 60.

TO MY DEAR BROTHER

JAMES,

I Dedicate this Little Book

AS A FAINT TOKEN OF GRATITUDE FOR THE LOVE THAT
A WHOLE LIFETIME OF DEVOTION WOULD
NOT BE SUFFICIENT TO REPAY.

THE AUTHOR.

Very Truly Yours
O V B Bozyd

PREFACE.

I TAKE pleasure in directing attention to the
kind and affectionate tribute paid my husband,
Captain Orsemus Bronson Boyd, and contained
in the Appendix of this volume. It is from the
pen of a former classmate, the gifted writer,
Colonel Richard Henry Savage.

I trust my readers will not think this introduction too lengthy. The perusal of it seems
necessary to a proper understanding of my
reasons for describing, in the following pages,
the pains, perils, and pleasures experienced by
land and sea in the various peregrinations of a
cavalry officer's wife. With Colonel Savage's
testimonial it furnishes a completeness to the
narrative that would otherwise be lacking.

In 1861, when every heart, both North and
South, was fired by military ardor, two brothers,

1

named Amos and Orsemus Boyd, lived in the small town of Croton, Delaware County, New York State. Immediately on the declaration of civil war they experienced but one desire — to join the Northern Army. The brothers had lost their mother when very young, but the stepmother their father had given them always endeavored to faithfully fill her place.

Additions to the family circle of a tiny boy and girl had only cemented its happy relations. Amos and his brother were, however, at the ages when boys welcome any escape from a life of wearisome monotony. Farm life, with its endless routine of seed-time and harvest, stretched before them a barren horizon. But neither was old enough to enlist without his father's sanction. Amos was less than eighteen years of age, and his brother but sixteen. Months passed before the father could be persuaded to give even a reluctant consent to the fervid desire of his sons to join the army. Finally it was gained, though he afterward sorely repented, and begged his wife to also spare him from her side, that he might accompany his boys. He could not endure the thought of his youthful sons departing for the scenes of such dangers without his sheltering presence.

By what means Mrs. Boyd was induced to consent to her husband's enlistment can only be understood by those who recall the loyal sentiments expressed by women in 1861. Our country was then aglow with patriotism. As in the South women gave their nearest and dearest to the cause, so in the North they were bereft of fathers, husbands, sons and brothers. In the little town of Croton every family sent at least one representative to the army, and many waved adieu to all its male members. This left to women the severe tasks of cultivating farms and rearing families.

The young stepmother of the lads in question not only lent her husband to his country, but during the entire three years of his absence tilled and tended the farm, and so well, that on his return it had not only improved in appearance, but also increased in value.

It requires little imagination to picture the sad parting when father and sons, after having enlisted in the Eighty-ninth Regiment New York Volunteers, left the quiet little village to join the army.

The younger son was not at first permitted to act as a soldier on account of his youth. Allowed to carry the flag at the head of the command, his bravery and boldness caused his father incessant anxiety. At the battle of Camden, when the second color bearer fell, our young hero seized his flag and carried that also until the close of battle. For such an act of bravery General Burnside summoned him to headquarters, and sent him home on recruiting service.

Prior to this young Boyd had been with Burnside's expedition off Cape Hatteras, where for twenty-six days the soldiers had lain outside, shipwrecked, and obliged to subsist on raw rice alone, as no fires could be built. When they finally landed on Roanoke Island our young lads were jubilant.

Orsemus took an active part in raising the One Hundred and Forty-fourth New York Volunteers, and for numberless acts of bravery was commissioned second lieutenant of Company D, September, 1862. By reason of the senior officers' absence he was for months, though but eighteen years of age, in command of a company of soldiers in which his father and elder brother were enlisted men. Perhaps no incident, even in those stirring war times, was more unusual.

The young lieutenant's father spent much time and effort in endeavoring to restrain his young son's ardor and ambition, which if unchecked would no doubt have resulted either in rapid promotion or an early grave. The lad knew no fear, and was always in the front of battle. His name was again and again mentioned in " General Orders " for "meritorious conduct."

Sadder than their home leaving was the return, two years later, of father and youngest boy, who went back to lay the remains of their eldest son and brother in the grave beside his mother. Amos had served his country well, and met the fate of many other brave soldiers.

In addition to this sorrow the father constantly feared lest his second son should also experience a soldier's death ; and while the father's heart glowed with pride at the encomiums lavished upon his boy's bravery, and the merited rewards it had already received, yet the fear of losing him was strongest, and at that home coming a compromise was effected.

The member of Congress from their district, desirous of finding an acceptable appointee to West Point, chose the gallant young lieutenant, who unwillingly accepted. Two years of active service had proved his essential fitness for the profession of arms.

With a heart burdened with sorrow, and yet not entirely hopeless, the father of two brave sons returned alone to his regiment, and finished three years of service with our noble Army of the Potomac.

Orsemus Boyd entered West Point in June, 1863, after having spent a short time in preparation. No doubt his years of service at the front had given the lad ideas at variance with the whims of those young men who had already passed their first year at the academy.

Any one who has been at West Point knows that a newly appointed cadet, or " plebe " as he is called, is expected not only to bow before his superior officers in the line of duty, but is compelled to endure all slights and snubs that any cadet chooses to impose. In 1863 the discipline in that respect was excessive.

The result, in the case of Mr. Boyd, was that he became unpopular for refusing to submit to many annoyances. The climax was reached when, after having fought with one cadet and come out the victor, he refused — having demonstrated his courage and ability — to fight with another, a man who had criticised the language used in the heat of battle, and was consequently dubbed a coward. This, though exceedingly trying to a person of his sensitive nature, was endured with the same patience as were subsequent trials.

After the furlough year, which comes when
the first long two years of cadet life have passed,
Mr. Boyd returned to West Point from that
most desired leave of absence, with renewed
hope and courage. Two months spent in his
boyhood's home, cheered and strengthened by
the love of many friends, enabled him to go
back animated by fullest intentions to ignore all
disagreeables and calmly prepare for a life of
usefulness. But it was not to be.

Shortly after Mr. Boyd's return he missed
sums of money brought from home, but said
nothing about it, as he had few confidants and
was naturally reticent.

In the same class with Mr. Boyd was a man
who had entered West Point at the avowed age
of twenty-five, though undoubtedly much older,
as his appearance indicated. During war time
the extreme of age for admission there, which
before and since was and is limited to twenty-
two years, had been extended to twenty-five.
This was done in order to permit young men
who had achieved distinction in real warfare

the opportunity of acquiring a military education. So this man, named Casey, had entered at the acknowledged age of twenty-five.

He was absolutely impecunious, and belonged to an Irish family in very humble circumstances. Mr. Boyd's parents, whose ancestors had fought in the Revolutionary War, were of pure and unadulterated American origin. Yet the superior age and cunning of the elder man unfitted the younger to cope with him. Always open and above board, Mr. Boyd neither knew nor expected tricks of any kind, and hence was not prepared to meet them.

Mr. Casey was compelled to procure money at all hazards. Before entering West Point he had married. That fact, if known, would have dismissed him at once from the academy, in accordance with the laws governing that institution, which permit no cadet to marry. It therefore became the object of Casey's life to conceal all knowledge of that which, if known, would have proved a potent factor in his downfall. Consumed with ambition and the desire to reach distinction in every social way, he assiduously cultivated the acquaintance of all cadets who could in any manner help him upward.

In the academy at that time were several cadets, sons of very wealthy parents, who, contrary to West Point rules, kept in their rooms at barracks large sums of money. That was Casey's opportunity, for he had constant need of it with which to silence the wife who had threatened his exposure. So great was the confidence of the academy classmates in each other that the money was simply placed in a trunk, to which all the clique had free access, and used as a general fund.

Government supplies cadets with all necessary articles, therefore only luxuries need be purchased, and the limit of these is much reduced by the absence of stores. So even to those generous young men the disappearance of money in large sums became puzzling, and led to inquiries which developed into suspicions, and a plan was formed to mark some of the bills, and thus discover the evil-doer. Mr. Boyd, by reason of his unpopularity, was unaware of these movements, and he had told no one of his own losses.

The cadets had informed their immediate commandant that money was constantly being stolen in the corps. Aghast at such a state of affairs, he had authorized and selected a committee of eight — two from among the eldest members of each company — to find and punish the thief. In an unguarded moment the commandant had said:

"If you find the offender, you can deal with him as you deem advisable."

The most prominent member of the committee was Casey, himself the real culprit. After a perfunctory search through quarters occupied by other cadets, they reached Mr. Boyd's, and found nothing to reward their efforts. At that juncture Casey glanced upward at a pile of books lying on some shelves, and said:

"Let us look in that large dictionary."

None but a crowd of frantic boys could have

failed to have observed how promptly he had selected the veritable book in which the money was found, where subsequent events, as well as his dying confession, proved he had himself placed it.

Casey's room, shared with Cadet Hamilton, was directly opposite that occupied by Mr. Boyd, who roomed alone because of his unpopularity. Mr. Boyd's room was so unguarded and accessible, that no doubt Casey had frequently entered it and taken money from the man whom he now accused. Casey had skillfully sought to direct suspicion in every way toward Mr. Boyd. Long had he wielded his baleful influence, to which, though no one had observed it, all had succumbed.

The search took place at noon, when the main body of the corps were at dinner. On Mr. Boyd's return to his room he found it filled with cadets, who madly accused him of the crime. White with horror and shame unspeakable, he answered their charges in a way which would have convinced any judge of human

nature that he was entirely innocent. Sinking
to his knees, and raising his eyes to heaven, he
said:

"By the memory of my dead mother I swear
I know nothing whatever of this money!"

To any one who knew the young man's
tender, brave soul, and how hallowed was the
memory of his mother, that avowal would have
sufficed. But it was not an occasion for calm
and deliberate judgment. The supposed culprit had at last been found, and he was in the
hands of Philistines. No thought of mercy im-
pelled any of those young men to hesitate in
their cruelty. With brute force — eight men
to one man — they placed Mr. Boyd in confine-
ment until later in the day, when at dress
parade they could publicly and brutally dis-
grace him.

I now quote, from a published account by an
eye-witness, the scene which followed:

"It was a cold, sad, lusterless day. The air
was full of snow and the cold was bitter.
Orders were given to fall into ranks in the area

of barracks for undress parade. The cadet adjutant commanded: ' Parade Rest.' After a pause he continued: ' Cadet captains will place themselves opposite their respective company fronts, and arrest any man who leaves the ranks.'

" There was an interval of the most profound stillness. Then above the wind's howling came the sound of tramping feet. Across the broad porch of the barracks and down the steps came four cadets, bearing between them a man's form. They advanced along the battalion's front. As they turned, the adjutant raised his right hand, and forthwith the drums and fifes beat and wailed out, in unmelodious and unearthly harmony, the terrible tune of the ' Rogue's March.'

" On they came ; and now I saw affixed to that man's breast a large white placard, and on it the words: ' COWARD !' ' LIAR !' ' THIEF !' The face above the words was marble white as the face of the dead, but the wild, staring, blood-red eyes seemed to wail and shrink in their horrible misery.

" The four cadets passed along the full length of the battalion, and with their victim turned down the slope beyond the buildings and disappeared."

On their way to the South Dock the persecuted man broke away from his accusers, but was warned to " beware " how he " ever set foot

again upon West Point," and threatened with
yet worse treatment should he do so.

General Cullom was then in command at
West Point.   On that particular evening he
was returning from the direction of the dock
toward which those heartless cadets had driven
Mr. Boyd, when he met the young man face to
face.   Amazed at the temerity of a cadet who
could boldly face him in civilian's attire, he
halted and said:

"What do you mean, sir?   Return at once to
your quarters!"

The general's first and most natural thought
was that Mr. Boyd had dressed himself in civilian's clothes, and was stealing off the post in
search of amusement.   But a second glance
showed him a face full of grief and shame — a
countenance on which utter woe was depicted.
He took the young man at once to his own
quarters, questioned him, and found to his dismay that the cadets had perpetrated a most un-
precedented and cruel outrage.

General Cullom determined then and there

that the matter should be sifted to the bottom. Mr. Boyd was to be tried, and proven either guilty or guiltless. His father was sent for, and the son allowed to return home pending the investigation.

What greater sorrow can be imagined than that which then fell upon this sorely stricken family? A young man who had faced the enemy's fire again and again, who had already won his shoulder-straps in the very front of war's alarms, to be charged with petty thievery, untruth, and cowardice! His stepmother said :

"Had our son been accused of fighting hastily, perhaps too readily, I could have believed him guilty. But for the sake of money Orsemus never could have done wrong."

Mr. Boyd had been supplied by his father with all the money he wanted, and at his own request an account kept of it, which showed that before this episode he had spent three hundred dollars — a large sum in a place like West Point, where every need is supplied by government.

The court of inquiry instituted by General Cullom resulted in a verdict of "not guilty." In the eyes of the cadets, whose insensate cruelty had warped their judgment, it was simply a Scotch verdict of "not proven;" and, though acquitted, the defendant was thenceforth a disgraced and dishonored man.

Mr. Boyd remained at the academy nearly two years longer, until his graduation in June, 1867. During all that time he was completely ostracized, and, with one, or possibly two exceptions, never exchanged one word with any cadet, all of whom regarded him as a coward. But none can contemplate such a life without marveling at its wonderful courage. Mr. Boyd had determined to graduate with honor, and thus show the world that he possessed such bravery as would not allow false charges to ruin his whole career.

I was introduced to him in 1866, and before our meeting had heard the whole story. The first look into his frank and manly countenance made me from that moment his stanch and true advocate. I was then attending school in New York, but finished in July, and we were married in October, three months after Mr. Boyd graduated.

Then began the hardships born of that West Point episode. Of course such bitter and terrible wrongs could not have been done a sensitive man without their affecting his whole life. To this may be attributed Mr. Boyd's desire to go West, and there remain.

It engendered in him a great unwillingness to demand even his just dues; and when he was ordered to leave California at a day's notice, and given no proper transportation, he submitted without a murmur. As I shared all those hardships, and shall always feel their effects, I have no hesitancy in saying that I attribute them all to the West Point wrong and injury.

Mr. Boyd could have entered the artillery branch of the service had he not longed to escape all reminders of that terrible experience, and so chose the Eighth Cavalry, which was stationed on the Pacific coast.

The subsequent hardships endured were due not only to the crude state of affairs at the West in those days, but also to the crushed spirit which so much injustice had engendered in my husband. He could not bear to ask favors, and be, perhaps, refused. Mr. Boyd even shrank at first from his fellow-officers. I know that no enlisted man's wife was ever exposed to more or severer perils than was the young school-girl from New York City; and I consider them the direct result of those sad years at West Point.

Mr. Boyd was always selected in after-years to handle the funds at every post where we were stationed, which distinctly showed how his honor was regarded by men competent to judge. But it resulted in countless expeditions that were both hazardous and expensive. He was sent by General Pope to build Fort Bayard because of his incorruptible honesty; but to be so constantly changing stations added greatly to our hardships.

" Vengeance is mine; I will repay, saith the

Lord." A singular evidence of the truth and justice of this text is shown in the meting out to those eight misguided young men of sorrow, misery, and sudden death, which seems to me a return for their attempted sacrifice of the career and honor of a gallant and innocent man. The roll is a terrible one. Casey, after confessing his crime, concealed it, aided and abetted by Hamilton. In less than a year after his apparently honorable graduation, he was shot by one of his own soldiers. Of the remainder, two committed suicide, one was murdered, one butchered by Modoc Indians; while family sorrow, bankruptcy, and disappointment or untimely death have caused the rest to mournfully regret their early hastiness and error of judgment, and the acts of gross cruelty which sprang therefrom.

THE AUTHOR.

CAVALRY LIFE.

CHAPTER I.

WHETHER or not these personal reminiscences will interest the public remains to be determined; for one thing the narrator can vouch, and that is they are not in the least exaggerated. Several army experiences have of late been printed, and when in recounting mine I have often been asked to write them, it was not, as I then thought, for the purpose of publication; although, as they have been unusual, to say the least, I have been tempted to do so; and now that the whole course of my life has been changed I have reasons for issuing this book which may perhaps plead my excuse should the narrative prove uninteresting to some.

21

The army world, though a small one, yet extends over a large amount of territory. My experience of it, previous to marriage, consisted in seeing, entirely at its best, beautiful West Point, which I considered a fair type of every army post; so when I married, immediately after his graduation from there, a young second lieutenant, I thought that however far we might travel such a home would always be found at our journey's end.

My husband, previous to his four years at West Point, as narrated in the preface, had been a soldier for two years in the War of the Rebellion, where he had so signalized himself by bravery that friends united in urging his father to remove the lad from the perilous surroundings of active warfare, and permit him to be educated in the profession for which he had shown such a decided talent. He was at that time but eighteen years old, and was probably the only man of that age who ever commanded a company in which his father and brother were enlisted men.

Mr. Boyd's previous career causing him to prefer the cavalry branch of the service, application was therefore made for that; so when appointed he was ordered to San Francisco. Not knowing whence from there he would be sent, as some of the companies of his regiment were in Nevada, some in Arizona, and others in California, it was deemed unwise for me to accompany him, so I remained in New York.

We had been married but two days, and it seemed to me as if San Francisco was as far away as China, particularly as there was then no trans-continental railroad. Besides, I had lived in New York City all my life, and considered it the only habitable place on the globe.

When Mr. Boyd reached San Francisco he was assigned to a station in Nevada, which was so remote, and there appeared to be so little hope for any comfortable habitation, that he wrote me the prospect for my journey was very indefinite.

However, with the hopefulness of youth, he counted on a far more speedy accomplishment of his desires than anything in the nature of the situation seemed to warrant. The troops had been sent, as a sort of advance guard and protective force for the contemplated Pacific Railroad, to a point in the very eastern part of Nevada. The camp was named "Halleck," in honor of General Halleck, and the accommodations were so limited that ladies were hardly needed, except to emphasize the limitations. Although it was well understood that I could not be comfortably located until summer, yet no second hint was needed when in mid-winter my husband wrote that I might come at least as far as San Francisco.

In the middle of January I left New York on one of the fine steamers of the Pacific Mail Steamship Company. The three weeks *en route* were delightful, and the change from bleak, cold winter to the tropical scenes of Panama, and thence to the soft and balmy air of the Pacific, was so exhilarating that travel was simply a continuous pleasure.

Upon reaching San Francisco, nothing seemed

more natural than that I should press on, in spite of the protestations of friends, who said that the Sierra Nevada Mountains were impassable at that season, and who predicted all sorts of mishaps. Nothing daunted, I determined at least to try, and so took steamer for Sacramento, and from thence train to Cisco, at the foot of the mountains, and the then terminus of the Pacific Railway. After leaving the train we continued our journey on sleds, in the midst of a blinding snowstorm, that compelled us to envelop our heads in blankets.

The snow, however, did not last many miles, and we were soon transferred to the regular stage-coach, a large vehicle with thorough-braces instead of springs, and a roomy interior which suggested comfort. Alas ! only suggested ! Possibly no greater discomfort could have been endured than my companion and self underwent that night. Those old-fashioned stage-coaches for mountain travel were intended to be well filled inside, and well packed outside. But it so happened that instead of the usual full complement of passengers, one other woman and myself were all.

A pen far more expert than mine would be required to do justice to the horrors of that night. Though we had left Cisco at noon, we did not reach Virginia City, on the other side of the mountains, until ten o'clock next morning. As long as daylight lasted we watched in amazement those wonderful mountains, which should have been called "Rocky," for they have enormous precipices and rocky elevations at many points; from the highest we gazed down into ravines at least fifteen hundred feet below, and shuddered again and again.

One point, called Cape Horn, a bold promontory, is famous, and as great a terror to stage-drivers as is the cape from which it takes its name to navigators. We peered into endless precipices, down which we momentarily expected to be launched, for the seeming recklessness of our driver and extreme narrowness of the roads made such a fate appear imminent.

Our alarm did not permit us to duly appreciate the scenery's magnificent grandeur; besides, every possible effort was required to keep from being tossed about like balls. We did not expect to find ourselves alive in the morning, and passed the entire night holding on to anything that promised stability. An ordinary posture was quite impossible: we had either to brace ourselves by placing both feet against the sides of the vehicle, or seize upon every strap within reach.

Long before morning all devices, except the extreme one of lying flat on the bottom of the coach and resigning ourselves to the inevitable, had failed. Every muscle ached with the strain that had been required to keep from being bruised by the constant bumping, and even then we had by no means escaped.

We had supped at Donner Lake, a beautiful spot in the very heart of the mountains, made famous by the frightful sufferings of the Donner party, which had given the lake its name, and which has been so well described by Bret Harte in "Gabriel Conroy," that a passing mention will suffice. It proved an unfortunate prelude to our eventful night; for in the midst of our own sufferings we were compelled to think of what might befall us if we, like that ill-fated party, should be left to the mercy of those grand but cruel mountains, which already seemed so relentless in their embrace that although haste meant torture yet we longed to see the last of them.

The bright sun shone high overhead long before we reached Virginia City, where I saw for the first time a real mining town. It is not my purpose to describe what has been so ably done by others, but simply confine myself to personal experiences; and I will, therefore, merely state that I gladly left Virginia City, knowing that soon after we should emerge from mountain roads, and on level plains be less tortured.

We were not, however, quite prepared for the method that made jolting impossible, and which, being the very extreme of our previous night's journey, was almost equally unendurable. On leaving the breakfast-table at Virginia

City, we were greatly surprised to find our coach almost full of passengers; but we climbed in, and for five days and nights were carried onward without the slightest change of any sort. There was a front and back seat, and between the two a middle one, which faced the back that we occupied. Whenever in the course of the succeeding five days and nights it was needful to move even our feet, we could only do so by asking our *vis-à-vis* to move his at the same time, as there was not one inch of space unoccupied.

The rough frontiersmen who were our fellow-passengers tried in every way to make our situation more endurable. After we had sat bolt upright for two days and nights, vainly trying to snatch a few moments' sleep, which the constant lurching of the stage rendered impossible, the two men directly facing us proposed, with many apologies, that we should allow them to lay folded blankets on their laps, when, by leaning forward and laying our heads on the rests thus provided, our weary brains might find some relief. We gratefully assented, only to find, however, that the unnatural position rendered sleep impossible, so decided to bear our hardships as best we could until released by time.

Our only respite was when the stage stopped for refreshments; but as we experienced all the mishaps consequent upon a journey in mid-winter, such as deep, clinging mud, which made regular progress impossible, we frequently found that meals were conspicuous by their absence; or we breakfasted at midnight and dined in the early morning. The food was of the sort all frontier travelers have eaten — biscuits almost green with saleratus, and meats sodden with grease, which disguised their natural flavors so completely that I often wondered what animals of the prairies were represented.

The names of our stopping-places were pretentious to such a degree that days passed before I was able to believe such grand titles could be personated by so little. I also noticed that a particularly forbidding exterior, and interior as well, would be called by the most high sounding name.

Alas for my hopes of escape from mountain travel! How gladly would I have welcomed some mountains instead of the endless monotony of that prairie! Nevada is particularly noted for the entire absence of trees, and the presence of a low, uninteresting shrub called sage-brush. It looks exactly as the name indicates, is a dingy sage-green in color, and, with the exception of a bush somewhat darker in hue and called grease-wood because it burns so readily, nothing else could be seen, not only for miles and miles, but day after day, until the weary eye longed for change. At dusk imagination compelled me to regard those countless bushes as flocks of sheep, so similar did they appear in the dim light, and I was unable to divest my mind of that idea during our entire stay in Nevada.

With such a state of affairs sleep was out of the question, and consequently nights seemed endless. I considered myself fortunate in having an end seat, and often counted the revolutions of the wheels until they appeared to turn more and more slowly, when I would propound that frequent query which always enraged the driver:

" How long before we reach the next station? "

I remember one night we made eight miles in fifteen hours, and the next day fifteen miles in eight hours. Both seemed wearily slow; but according to our driver the roads were to blame.

That night the monotony was relieved by what we considered a very pleasing incident, as it afforded some excitement. A rather small pig decided to accompany us, and some of the passengers made our driver frantic by betting on piggy winning the race: as a fact, he did reach the station first. I felt quite dejected at having to leave him there; for in our lonely journey we longed for companions in misery, and he seemed very miserable during that weary night.

Notwithstanding the level monotony of the country, we were constantly being brought up short by gullies which crossed our road. The sensation was akin to that one experiences when arrested by the so-called "thank-you-mums," met with in Eastern rural districts.

As the very tiniest streams in the West are designated rivers, we were always expecting, only to be disappointed, great things in that line. At last, when we reached Austin, and saw that the Reese River could be stepped across, all expectations of future greatness in the way of rivers were relinquished.

Austin, at that time a very small mining town, was so insignificant as to be regarded as merely a mile-stone on the journey. We gladly left it to continue our travels, which soon became less monotonous by reason of low mountains that we crossed in the night, before reaching what I had hoped was to be the end of my long stage-ride.

Mr. Boyd had arrived first at the military camp at Ruby, where we remained two days to rest before continuing our journey. This was necessary, as the loss of sleep for five long nights had so prostrated me that when I found myself in a recumbent position, consciousness to all outside surroundings was so completely lost that the intervening day and night were entirely blotted out.

I no longer felt particularly young. Experience and the loss of sleep had aged me. Yet knowing that the years which had passed over my head were as few as were consistent with the dignity of a married woman, I was taken quite aback when one of the employees connected with the stage station asked my husband:

"How did the old woman stand the trip?"

I listened intently for his answer, fully expecting to hear the man severely rebuked, if not laid flat; but Mr. Boyd understood human nature better than I, and in the most polite tones replied:

"Thank you, very well indeed."

We were then within about one hundred miles of our destination, Fort Halleck, Nevada, and the remainder of our journey was to be

made in an entirely different vehicle from the
stage-coach — a government ambulance, and
in this case the most uncomfortable one I have
ever seen. Many are delightful; but that was
an old, worthless affair, and instead of the usual
comfortable cross seats had long side ones, which
covered with slippery leather made security of
position impossible. My trunk was first placed
inside, then a huge bundle of forage, which left
only room for two people near the door.

We jogged on monotonously the first day,
seeing the same scenery: it seemed to me a
duplicate of that looked upon for days past.
Very thankful I was, however, for the absence
of any steep hills; for we fully expected, at the
first climb, to be buried under my own huge
trunk, which appeared to have as great a tendency to shift its position as I had.

Instead of feeling a womanly pride in the
possession of an abundant wardrobe, I ruefully
wished most of it had been left behind, more
especially as the stage company charged a dollar
for each pound of its weight. The combined

amount of this and my stage fare was just two hundred and fifty dollars. As my fare by steamer had been exactly that amount, I had, before reaching my husband, disposed of five hundred dollars, in return for which five seemingly endless days and sleepless nights of tiresome travel had been endured, together with many bumps and bruises.

One of the objects I have in writing these adventures is to show how an army officer is compelled to part with all he obtains from the government in paying expenses incurred by endless journeys through newly settled countries.

But to resume our ambulance trip. As night approached the motion ceased, and I doubt if mortal was ever more amazed than I when told we were to go no farther. Not a sign of habitation was in sight! Nothing but broad plains surrounded us on all sides! Not even a tree could be seen, and the four mules had to be hitched to our ambulance wheels, as tiny bushes were not, of course, available for such a purpose. A fire was made of grease-wood, a piece

of bacon broiled on the coals, and a huge pot of
coffee served in quart tin cups, which is the
only way soldiers condescend to drink it, as no
less amount will suffice, coffee being their greatest solace on long marches.

That, my first real experience in camping out,
was indeed novel. The knowledge that except
one tiny dot in the wilderness — our ambulance
— we had no resting-place, gave me a curiously
homeless feeling that was indeed cheerless.

When, a little later, we sought our couch, it
proved to be anything but downy. My trunk
and the forage had been taken out, and the
seats, always made as in a sleeping-car so that
the backs let down, formed the bed. It was
not, however, altogether uncomfortable, as we
had plenty of blankets.

Soon after falling asleep I was awakened by
what seemed to be a complete upheaval of our
couch. I was thoroughly terrified and prepared for almost anything; but examination
showed that our alarm was caused by one of
the mules, that had worked his way under our

ambulance, and in attempting to rise had almost upset it. A readjustment of the lines by which a mule was tied to each wheel somewhat reassured me; but those playful attempts to either upset or drag our extemporized couch in any direction in which the mules felt inclined to go, resulted in our passing a restless night. Sometimes one mule would be seized with an ambitious desire to break away; this would rouse the other three, who would each in turn attempt to stampede, and but for the driver's timely assistance it is difficult to state what might have happened, as our vehicle was not sufficiently strong to withstand such violent wrenches.

When morning dawned we resumed our march, and great was my joy on learning that we would have four walls around us during the two succeeding nights. I was, however, rather startled to find myself disturbing so many that evening, for when we reached the little log hut that was to shelter us, it proved to be, though but eighteen feet square, the abode of ten men.

In all the log cabins at which we stopped a bed occupied one corner of their only room. Those beds were, of course, only rough bunks of un-planed pine timber; but by reason of being raised above the mud floors formed very desirable resting-places.

The almost chivalrous kindness of frontiersmen has become proverbial with women who have traveled alone in the far West, where the presence of any member of the sex is so rare the sight of one seems to remind each man that he once had a mother, and no attention which can be shown is ever too great. When, therefore, our hosts saw my reluctance to deprive them of what must have been occupied by at least two of their number, they assured me I would confer a favor by accepting the proffered hospitality. Although shrinking from the proximity of so many men, yet remembering my shaky bed of the previous night, I was glad to find refuge behind the improvised curtains which they deftly arranged.

It seemed indeed odd on this and succeeding

nights to see huge, stalwart men preparing food, baking the inevitable biscuits in Dutch ovens over the coals in open fireplaces, and being so well pleased if we seemed to enjoy what was placed before us.

Our next day's journey was diversified by the discovery that our vehicle was like the famous one-horse shay, likely to drop in pieces ; indeed, we had twice to send back several miles for the tires, which had parted company with their wheels. Such a condition of our conveyance, coupled with several other mishaps, led us to feel very dubious as to our destination being eventually reached in safety.

On arriving at the cabin in which our third night was to be passed, we found it occupied by fifteen men. As usual, we were ensconced in the only bed. I tried to feel doubly protected, instead of embarrassed, by the vicinity of so many men ; nor did I consider it necessary to peer about in an effort to learn how they disposed of themselves. I well knew it was too cold to admit of any sleeping outside. Being startled by some noise in the night, I drew back the curtains, and looked on a scene not soon to be forgotten. Not only were the men ranged in rows before us, but the number of sleepers had been augmented by at least six dogs, which had crept in for shelter from what I found in the morning was a severe snow-storm, that covered the ground to the depth of ten inches or more.

On the last day of that long journey I arose, feeling particularly happy at the prospect of soon reaching our destination ; and even the sight of snow did not disconcert me, as I reasoned that we were to ride in a covered vehicle, and with only twenty miles to traverse had nothing to fear.

Though all might have gone well had our ambulance been strong, but two miles of the distance had been covered when we sank in an enormous snow-drift. Our mules had wandered from the road into a deep gully, and in trying to pull us out succeeded in extricating only the front wheels of the wagon, so farther progress in that vehicle was quite impossible. Nothing could be done except call upon our friends of the past night for assistance, which they promptly rendered, sending us their only wagon — an open, springless one — which seemed so exposed they begged me to return to the cabin. But my anxiety to reach our journey's end was by that time so great I would have tried to walk could no other mode of procedure have been found.

So, seated in the very center of the wagon, with as much protection as our blankets could afford, we rode the remaining eighteen miles, snow falling continually and rendering it impossible to distinguish the road. Travel under such conditions, and especially in a springless conveyance, made our previous jaunt over mountains fade into insignificance.

The day seemed endless; and though at first I kept shaking off the snow, yet when we reached our destination, after riding for twelve long hours, I had become so worn and weary as to no longer care, and was almost buried beneath it.

It is always the last straw which breaks the
camel's back, and that, the last day of our journey, was the first on which I had felt discouraged; in spite of constant efforts I finally
succumbed to our doleful surroundings, and
in tears was lifted out and carried into what
proved to be my home for the next year.

CHAPTER II.

WHEN courage to look around had at last been mustered, I found that my new home was formed of two wall tents pitched together so the inner one could be used as a sleeping and the outer one as a sitting room. A calico curtain divided them, and a carpet made of barley sacks covered the floor. In my weary state of mind and body the effect produced was far from pleasant. The wall tents were only eight feet square, and when windowless and doorless except for one entrance, as were those, they seemed from the inside much like a prison.

As I lay in bed that night, feeling decidedly homesick, familiar airs, played upon a very good piano, suddenly sounded in my ears. It seemed impossible that there could be a fine musical instrument such a distance from civilization, particularly when I remembered the roads over which we had come, and the cluster of tents that alone represented human habitation. The piano, which I soon learned belonged to our captain's wife, added greatly to her happiness, and also to the pleasure of us all, though its first strains only intensified my homesick longings.

This lady and myself were the only women at the post, which also included, besides our respective husbands, the doctor and an unmarried first lieutenant. The latter, as quartermaster and commissary, controlled all supplies, and could make us either comfortable or the reverse, as he chose.

Shortly afterward another company of soldiers, embracing one married officer and two unmarried ones, joined us; but at first our troop of cavalry was all. The men, instead of living in tents, were quartered in dugouts, which, as their name implies, were holes dug in the ground, warm enough, but to my unaccustomed eyes places in which only animals should have been sheltered, so forbidding and dingy did they seem. The soldiers were not, however, destined to spend the summer in such accommodations, for by that time very comfortable barracks had been erected.

As everything in the life I then led was new and strange, and surroundings have always powerfully influenced me, I took note of many things which it seemed should have been remedied. One which greatly troubled me was the power extremely young officers exercised over enlisted men. If the latter were in the least unruly, most fearful punishment awaited them, which in my opinion was not commensurate with the offense, but depended entirely upon the mercy and justice of the offender's superior officer, who usually but a boy himself had most rigid ideas of discipline.

I have always noticed how years temper judgment with any one in authority, and thus have come to believe that no very young man is capable of wielding it. Situated as we were in tents, so the slightest sound could be heard, we were made aware of all that transpired outside. When an enlisted man transgressed some rule and was severely punished, I always became frantic, for his outcries reached my ears, and I recognized the injustice and impropriety of some mere boy exercising cruel authority over any man old enough to be his father.

Methods have completely changed in the army since that time, and I am glad to state that for many years past such scenes as then wrung my heart have been unknown; but in those days our military organization was so crude many things were permitted which are now scarcely remembered by any one. Our soldiers, recruited from the Pacific coast, then famous for the demoralized state of its poorer classes, were indeed in need of firm discipline; but it required men with more experience than those young officers possessed to wield it.

I always have had, and always shall have, a tender, sympathetic feeling for American soldiers. In fact, most of the kindly help which made life on the frontier endurable to me came from those men. We were never able to procure domestic help; it was simply out of the question, and for years it would have been necessary for me either to have cooked or starved but for their ever-ready service.

To cook in a modern kitchen, or even in an ancient one, is not so dreadful; but to cook amid the discomforts and inconveniences which surrounded me for many years would have been impossible to any delicately nurtured woman. I recall the delight with which an offer of help from a soldier in that, my first effort at housekeeping, was welcomed. Although I soon became the slave of my cook's whims, because of my utter inexperience and ignorance, yet his forethought when the floor was soaked with rain in always having a large adobe brick heated ready to be placed under my feet when dining, will never be forgotten.

The greatest proof of devotion I ever received was when that man, learning that the laundress declined longer employing her services in our behalf, saw me preparing to essay the task myself. To prevent that he rose sufficiently early to do the work, and continued the practice so long as we remained there, despite the fact that it subjected him to ridicule from other soldiers; and so sensitive was he in regard to the subject that I never unexpectedly entered the kitchen while he was ironing without noticing his endeavors to hastily remove all trace of such occupation.

As the season was severe — the thermometer during that and the succeeding winter frequently fell to thirty-three degrees below zero — a large stove had been placed in the outer tent, and a huge fireplace built in the inner one. A large pine bunk, forming a double bed, occupied nearly all the spare space, and left only just room enough in front of the fire to seat one's self, and also to accommodate the tiniest shelf for toilet purposes. It therefore required constant watchfulness to avoid setting one's clothing on fire; and among other ludicrous occurrences was the following:

In our inability to find suitable places for

necessary articles, we were apt to use most inappropriate ones. On the occasion referred to, a lighted candle had been placed on the bed, where my husband seated himself without noticing the candle. Soon arose the accustomed smell of burning, and I executed my usual maneuver of turning about in front of the fire to see if my draperies had caught. The odor of burning continued to increase, yet I could find no occasion for it.

The cause, however, was discovered when I leaned over the bed, and saw that a large hole had been burned in the center of Mr. Boyd's only uniform coat. He had been too intent on shielding me to be conscious of his own peril. It was an accident much to be regretted, for our isolation was so complete that any loss, however trifling, seemed irreparable by reason of our remoteness from supplies. A lengthened account of our difficulties in procuring needed articles during this and many subsequent years would seem incredible.

I had been delighted to purchase, at the stage

station where we stopped previous to our one hundred miles' ambulance trip, and for exactly the amount of one month's pay, a modest supply of dishes and cooking utensils. Prior to their arrival we were happy to obtain our meals at the house of the quartermaster's clerk; yet I looked eagerly forward to my first attempt at housekeeping, and daily sought to induce our quartermaster to send for the goods. At last he informed us that they were on the way, and then began tiresome efforts to have some sort of kitchen and dining-room prepared.

All my entreaties resulted only in a number of willows being stuck in the ground and covered with barley sacking. Even the door was composed of two upright and two cross pieces of willow covered with sacking; a simple piece of leather, which when caught on a nail served as fastening and handle, was deemed sufficient guard. The floor was primitive ground, and in time, as it became hardened by our feet, was smooth except where the water from above wore it into hollows. No efforts of mine could ever induce the powers that were to cover the roof so as to exclude rain. At first some old canvas was simply stretched over it; but as the roof was nearly flat this soon had to be replaced. By degrees, as cattle were killed for the soldiers, we used the skins which were otherwise valueless, lapping them as much as possible. However, they formed no effectual barrier to melting snow or falling rain, as later experience proved, when it became only an ordinary occurrence for me to change my seat half a dozen times during one meal.

Young people are not easily discouraged, and I was very happy when informed that our housekeeping goods had arrived and been placed in the quarters prepared for them. An ominous sound which greeted our ears as we opened the boxes rather dismayed us; but we were not prepared for the utter ruin that met our eyes. What had not been so brittle as to break, had been rendered useless and unsightly by having been chipped or cracked; and as we took out the last piece of broken ware I concluded that what

was left might be sold in New York for a dollar. On comparing the residue with the inven-
tory, we discovered that half the goods were
missing.

The articles had been bought from an army
officer who was changing stations, and were
not strictly what I should have chosen. Everything, however, was useful there, and I was
rather pleased that we had duplicates of nearly
every article, although results showed that this
had tempted the freighters' cupidity, and they
had fitted themselves out with the primary supply; so when by breakages the secondary disappeared, we had really nothing of any consequence left. Bitterness was added to sorrow,
when of a dozen tumblers only the *débris* of six
were found. The common kitchen ware was
too solid to be shattered, but everything at all
fragile was in fragments.

The triumph with which we evolved from
the chaos a large wash-bowl and pitcher, which
though in close proximity to a pair of flat-irons
had escaped injury, was equaled only by our

chagrin when we found our little toilet shelf too small to hold them, and were therefore obliged to return to a primitive tin basin, though hoping in time for enough lumber to build accommodations which would allow us the luxury of white ware.

I regret to state that the climate proved too much for our large pitcher. One morning we found it cracked from the cold to which it had been exposed in the out-door kitchen, in which we were obliged to keep it. Our basin was cherished; but on the anniversary of our wedding-day I nearly sank from mortification when Mr. Boyd came into our tent, which was filled with friends who had gathered to celebrate the occasion, carrying the wash-bowl full of very strong punch which he had concocted. No thought of apologizing for our lack of delicacies occurred to me, but I felt compelled to explain, in the most vehement fashion, that the wash-bowl had never been utilized for its obvious purpose; in fact, this was the first period of its usefulness.

My housekeeping was simplified by absolute lack of materials. I had, as a basis of supplies, during that and the succeeding two years, nothing but soldiers' rations, which consisted entirely of bacon, flour, beans, coffee, tea, rice, sugar, soap, and condiments. Our only luxury was dried apples, and with these I experimented in every imaginable way until toward the last my efforts to disguise them utterly failed, and we returned to our simple rations. I was unable to ring any changes on rice, for after Mr. Boyd's experience with General Burnside's expedition off Cape Hatteras, the very sight of it had become disagreeable to him.

We had at that time no trader's store within two miles, which was a matter of congratulation, for when we indulged our desire for any change of fare, however slight, we felt as if eating gold. Nothing on the Pacific coast could be paid for in greenbacks; only gold and silver were used; and when an officer's pay, received in greenbacks, was converted into gold, a premium of fifty per cent always had to be paid.

That, added to frontier prices, kept us poor and hungry for years. If we indulged in a dozen eggs the price was two dollars in gold. If we wanted the simplest kind of canned goods to relieve the monotony of our diet, the equivalent was a dollar in gold.

I had always disliked to offend any one ; but remarking one day that the flavor of wild onions which permeated the only butter we could procure, and for which we paid two dollars and a half a pound, was not exactly to our taste, seriously offended the person who made it. I quite rejoiced thereat when she refused to supply us with any more, feeling that a lasting economy had been achieved without any great self-denial. The taint of numerous kinds of wild herbs of all sorts, during the many years of my frontier life, always made both beef and milk as well as butter unpalatable, especially in the early spring season, and in Texas, where the flavor was abominable.

There were so many motives for economy that we rejoiced continually at our inability to procure supplies. First should be named the fact that a lieutenant's pay, exceedingly small at best, was, when converted into gold, just eighty dollars per month. That reality was augmented by an utter inequality in the cost of actual necessaries. We found, for instance, that we must have at least two stoves — one for cooking and the other for heating purposes. Their combined cost was one hundred and seventy-five dollars, although both could have been bought in New York for about twenty dollars. If we ever rebelled against such seeming impositions, the cost of freight would be alluded to ; and remembering what the expenses of my poor solitary trip had been we were effectually silenced.

Among the many amusing stories told on that subject, none was more frequently quoted in every frontier station than the retort of a Hebrew trader, who, when expostulated with on account of the exorbitant charge of a dollar for a paper of needles, vehemently replied :

"Oh, it is not de cost of de needles ! It is de freight, de freight ! "

So when obliged to purchase any article we counted its cost as compared with the freight as one to one hundred.

Shortly after we reached Camp Halleck, a team was sent to Austin for supplies; and being sadly in need of chairs it was decided that if we ordered the very strongest and ugliest kitchen ones they would escape injury, and be cheap. The bill was received before the team returned, and to our dismay we found that the six chairs cost just six dollars each in gold, or fifty dollars in greenbacks. We tried to hope they would be so nice that the price would prove of slight consequence. But lo! the teamster brought but one chair, and that a common, black, old-fashioned kitchen one.

When asked about the other five, the man replied that the roads were so bad, our chairs, having been placed on top of the load, were continually falling under the wheels, and finally, broken in pieces, had been left to their fate. We, however, suspected that they had served as firewood. We frequently joked, after the first

pangs had worn away, over our fifty-dollar chair,
claiming a great favor was bestowed upon any
one allowed to occupy it.

Reading matter was our only luxury, and the
weekly mail, always an uncertainty, was just as
apt to have been lightened of its contents in
transit, if the roads were at all heavy, as any
other package. We were never sure, therefore,
that we should be able to understand the next
chapters in serial stories, which were our
delight.

I remember being very much engrossed in one
of Charles Reade's novels, the heroine of which
was cast on a desert island, where I thought
only her lover's presence could reconcile her to
the absence of supplies. The story was published in *Every Saturday*, and at first came
weekly ; but after we had become most deeply
interested five weeks passed during which not
a single number was received, and we were left
to imagine the sequel.

Several periodicals of a more solid nature always came regularly, which fact constrained us

to believe that we were furnishing light literature to the poor inhabitants of some lonely stage station on the road; and in that belief we tried to find consolation for our own losses. Rumors of the outside world grow dim in such an isolated life: we were unwilling to become rusty, and hence read with avidity all printed matter that reached us.

There were, however, other diversions. I learned to play cribbage admirably; and as my husband was able to give me a good deal of his time we found it a pleasant pastime. The winter seemed well-nigh interminable, and we longed for snow to disappear, intending then to explore the whole country. I was such a novice in the saddle that the steadiest old horse, called " Honest John," was chosen for me ; and by the time pleasant weather had come I was ready to ride in any direction, having learned that my steed was all his name implied.

We found the streams, so small and insignificant during the dry season, enlarged by melting snows from the mountains; and they were not only beautiful, as clear running water ever is, but were filled with the most delicious spotted trout, which on our fishing-trips we caught and cooked on the spot, and whose excellence as food simply beggars description.

Though the country remained almost as dreary as in mid-winter, grass made some improvement. The lovely wild-flowers, in endless beauty and variety, were a ceaseless delight; while our camp, situated on a lovely little stream in a grove of cottonwood-trees, was far more beautiful than I had ever imagined it could be.

Unfortunately there were no trees to cast their shade over our tents; and as in mid-winter we had suffered from intense cold, so in summer we suffered from intense heat. The sun penetrated the thin canvas overhead to such an extent that my face was burned as if I had been continually out-of-doors, or even more so, as its reflected glare was most excessive. Then we were almost devoured by gnats so small that netting was no protection against them. I had never before, nor have I ever since, seen any insect in such quantities, nor any so troublesome and annoying.

In after-years I became accustomed to the most venomous creatures of all sorts, and in time learned not to mind any of them; but while in Nevada I endured tortures from a colony of wasps that took possession of the canvas over the ridge-poles which connected the uprights of our tents. At first we scarcely noticed them; but they must either have multiplied incredibly, or else gathered recruits from all directions, for soon they swarmed in countless numbers above our heads, going in and out through the knot-holes in our rough pine door, buzzing about angrily whenever we entered hastily — in fact, disputing possession with us to such a degree that I dared not open the door quickly. Whenever I did, one of the angry insects was sure to meet and sting me. They remained with us during the summer, and when we finally left were masters of the field by reason of their superior numbers.

I have often since wondered why we did not dispossess them by some means, as they were the terror of my life. One day while in the inner tent, where I felt safe, dressing for break- fast, I experienced the most intense sting on my ankle. The pain was so great I screamed, doubly frightened because confident a rattle- snake had bitten me, and too terrified to exer- cise any self-control. My cries soon brought a dozen or more persons to the scene, who found a wretched wasp, and calmed my fears ; but my nerves had been terribly shaken. Since then I have met army ladies who live in constant terror of snakes, tarantulas, and scorpions; though no longer sharing their fears, I always sympathize with them.

I soon became an expert fisher; and the dainty food thus procured was a great addition to our supplies. With all its drawbacks, life in the open air then began to have many charms for me.

We made friends with the neighboring ranch- men, particularly those who were married, as their wives interested us greatly, they were such perfect specimens of frontier women. At first the rancheros were a little shy, but soon made us welcome to their homes and festivities, where we were always urged to remain as long as possible. Gradually new arrivals — always called " sister " or " cousin " — appeared at several of the ranches, and soon a rumor gained ground that though not exactly in Utah, the Mormon religion prevailed to some extent in our locality.

Another source of great interest was the Piute and Shoshone Indians, who were so numerous that I soon regarded red men as fearlessly as if I had been accustomed to them all my life. They were deeply interested in us, at times inconveniently so; for they never timed their visits, but always came to stay, and would frequently spend the entire day watching our movements.

In one of their camps, several miles away, I found a beautiful dark-eyed baby boy, to whom I paid frequent visits, which were at first well received. But one day I carried the child a neat little dress — my own handiwork — and before arraying baby in it gave him a bath, which evidently caused his mother to decide that I had sinister designs upon her prize, for on my subsequent visits no trace of the baby could ever be found. Had his sex been different I probably could have obtained complete possession; but boys are highly prized among the Indians.

We considered ourselves well repaid for a ride of twenty miles by an Indian dance. It was, of course, only picturesque at night, when seen by the light of huge fires; then, indeed, the sight was weird and strange! On such an occasion, when depicting so perfectly their warfare, the Indians seemed to return to their original savage natures. Had it not been for our fully armed escort we might have feared for safety.

It was startling to see the Indians slowly circle around their camp-fire, at first keeping time to a very slow, monotonous chant, which by degrees increased in volume and rapidity, until finally their movements became fast and furious, when savagery would be written in every line of their implacable countenances. I could then realize in some degree how little mercy would be shown us should they once become inimical; but seeing them at all times so thoroughly friendly made it difficult to think of them as otherwise; and therefore, when we afterwards lived among the most savage tribes, I never experienced that dread which has made life so hard for many army ladies.

With the advent of early spring active preparations were made to build houses for the officers before the ensuing winter. We watched their slow progress, hoping against hope that we might occupy one of the cozy little dwellings. All sorts of difficulties, however, seemed to delay their construction, for good workmen were as scarce as good food, and we found that while anticipation and expectation were pleasing fancies, realization was but a dream. All our hopes were doomed to disappointment, for we finally left the post on the following January, just one year after my arrival, with the house we had longed to occupy still unfinished ; thus I passed half of the second winter in our two small tents.

CHAPTER III.

MEANTIME much had happened to make that
year an eventful one.   My expectation of finding the new, untried world into which I was
ushered a place where all were ready to meet
me with open hearts and hands had been completely shattered.   The captain who commanded
our company, and the first lieutenant, had taken
a violent dislike to Mr. Boyd because he was
unaccustomed to the lack of discipline they
allowed; and their almost unlimited powers enabled them to deprive us of much to which we
were justly entitled.

They were two of the most illiterate men
whom I have ever met; and shortly after, when
the army consolidated, both found more fitting
occupation in a frontier mining town.   I mention this only to account for the unnecessary

hardships to which we were subjected. For instance, when gardens were planted, and the company was raising fine vegetables, we were allowed neither to buy nor to use any, and had to continue to live on rations.

But the most unkind treatment of all was shown when my husband met with a severe accident. He was returning from a successful fishing-trip when his horse — and a more unruly mustang cannot well be imagined — fancied some cause for fright, and began to buck on the side of a steep hill. Mr. Boyd, deeming discretion the better part of valor, jumped off, and fell with his entire weight upon one leg, fracturing it just below the knee. His companion decided to ride into camp, a distance of six miles, for assistance, and a litter was at once sent out. My husband lay there alone, helpless and suffering, until long after dark, the coyotes, or small wolves, coming around in droves, and it was with the greatest difficulty he kept them off by the use of both gun and pistol.

When he was brought into camp late at night,

my first remark was that I derived some comfort from the situation, inasmuch as he would not be compelled to join an expedition which had been for some time projected. Mr. Boyd was to have been sent with an escort of twenty men on a surveying party. That would have kept him in the field all summer, and left me entirely alone.

The officer in command displayed his malevolence by sending with the expedition the soldier who had volunteered to wait on us, thus leaving me without the slightest assistance in caring for my husband. The doctor was exceedingly kind and good, and I could obtain my meals where we had on my first arrival; but I was obliged to carry Mr. Boyd's food quite a long distance, and perform every sort of hard, menial labor — even chopping wood; for nights, lying unable to move, my husband would become chilly and need a fire.

Many other hardships were entailed, and I was quite worn out with working and nursing, when, in a month's time, Mr. Boyd was able to walk on crutches. However, the accident had given me his society for the entire summer, at which I rejoiced exceedingly ; for I had often wondered what I should do if left alone, friendless as I felt myself to be.

At that time the whole army was in a chaotic state, especially on the Pacific coast, where California volunteers, though brave and hardy men, were totally unaccustomed to military discipline, and the officers not of a character to enforce it. The wild lawlessness which had made California a place of terror, and that had only been subdued by the vigilance committee, was still extant, and many occurrences during our first year of army life showed there were desperadoes among us.

Had the officers in command been gentlemen, at least a semblance of respect would have been shown; but the enlisted men, treated by their officers exactly as they had been while both were volunteers, were disposed to dislike a man who after four years of rigid training at West Point had grown accustomed to discipline and was disposed to exact it.

The first duty which called my husband from home was an expedition after some horses that had been sent to Camp McDermott, a distance of about two hundred miles. He took with him ten men, and experienced very little difficulty in managing them while going; but returning, with twenty extra horses, the soldiers were in a lawless state, disposed to be unruly, and would become intoxicated whenever liquor could be had. Despite the fact that water was obtainable only at the stations *en route*, Mr. Boyd made a practice of procuring in casks all that would be needed, and marching a few miles beyond the stations, so as to prevent liquor being obtained; for in all those places, although water might be scarce, a barrel of the vilest whisky could always be found.

The plan worked well for the first hundred miles; but one night the men stole back to the station and insisted that liquor be given them. Mr. Boyd always warned station-masters of the extreme danger of allowing his men to have whisky, as with so many horses the services of all were required ; but that day some had been procured from an unknown source, and they were determined to have more. The station-master refused to furnish it, and barricaded his door so that no one could enter.

The men were infuriated; and just as my husband arrived on the scene one of them rushed madly against the door and forced it open, only to be met by a ball from a pistol fired by some one inside the room, which killed him instantly. That sobered the rest, who obeyed the order given to carry their dead comrade back to the encampment. Fearing further disturbance my husband broke camp and traveled till daylight, when finding the already over-loaded wagon much encumbered by the dead body, which had repeatedly slipped off, he stopped and buried it by the roadside. After that he had no trouble, as the men were completely subdued.

On their return to camp the entire story was related to me; and knowing how great Mr. Boyd's anxiety had been, I fully expected he would be commended, if not rewarded. Instead of that he was actually called to account, principally for burying the dead soldier by the roadside, which the commanding officer seemed to consider wrong, when to have traveled so many days with the body uncoffined would have been quite impossible.

I was highly diverted by the efforts my husband made to procure presents for me, and shall never forget the peculiarity of his gifts. In passing through Austin at one time he endeavored to buy fruit, as we missed it greatly, and deemed a box of apples at only one dollar a dozen a marvelous bargain, as three dollars had been paid for those previously purchased.

On another occasion Mr. Boyd had yielded to the temptation to buy a sewing-machine, which he thought would please me very much, as indeed it would had I been able to use it; but the machine was entirely out of order and represented nothing in the way of usefulness, unless a month's pay which it had cost might be so considered.

Another present was of a more noisy sort. Knowing that I had never seen a "burro," Mr. Boyd was induced to buy one for me because it was cheap and so docile a child might ride it. The latter it certainly proved to be ; but living in tents, where every sound penetrated to our ears, the animal became a perpetual nuisance ; consequently, when one day he strayed away, never to reappear, we were not sorry.

The brute was indeed small, but his voice was a marvel of strength and volume, and his bray resounded on all sides at the most inopportune moments. If military orders were being read, " Burro " kept up an accompaniment which drowned all other sounds ; and in his apparent loneliness, the poor fellow had a way of seeking human companionship, and would appear at our doorstep and lift up his voice in a manner that made us feel the roof must rise above our heads in order to allow the fearful sound to escape. He afforded us a great deal of amusement, however, and all his antics were laughed at and condoned.

About that time another troop of the regiment was sent from Idaho, and we then enjoyed the society of a very charming New York woman, who accompanied her husband, and the fittings of whose tent amused us much. This lady had a large private fortune, yet she had not been with us a month before, resigning herself to the inevitable, she bent weekly over the wash-tub and ironing-board, as help was not procurable; nor did this officer's wife find a treasure of a soldier, as I had, who would volunteer to relieve her of such unaccustomed drudgery.

Deciding that her tent would present a more cheerful appearance if papered, all newspapers received were, immediately after being read, pasted on the walls. A preference was given to illustrated journals, and it was very diverting to inspect those pictures which reflected many scenes of our former lives. How often the wish was expressed that we could be as well sheltered as were the servants in city homes, and my friend frequently longed for as good a roof overhead as had her mother's barn. A year of such hardships sufficed; at the end of that time her husband resigned his commission, and for many years they have been quartered in New York City.

As the second winter of our camp life approached, we prepared in a measure for it by procuring a larger heating stove; but the stove took up a great deal of room in our little tent, and so was crowded into a corner, with the result of constant danger from fire. I attempted to keep account of the number of times our tent had ignited and been patched to cover the burned places. Mr. Boyd usually built a fire very early, before going to his duties, and on one memorable morning the entire top of our sitting-room tent burned away, leaving it quite uncovered.

My anxiety to live in a house was so great that I calmly deliberated whether or not to call for assistance; but second thoughts concerning the probable destruction of our belongings, and the absurdity of expecting a house to immediately erect itself for our benefit, decided me. I had really grown inured to fire, as one would naturally become who was exempt from all personal danger; for if the canvas had burned away, open air and sky would have surrounded us.

During all those months work had been actively prosecuted on the Union Pacific Railroad; and as it was to approach us very closely, we felt that not only would personal benefit result therefrom, but it would bring an influx of inhabitants into the country which must promote its prosperity through opening mines, irrigating and cultivating arable land, and so forth. The latter, however, became problematical, as it was found impossible to procure other labor than Chinese on the railroad. The class of settlers who occasionally appeared were of a restless, nomadic sort; and if they located on a plot of land soon tired of the industry required to make of the place a home.

The chief result of the increased population was most noticeable in the number of accidents which occurred both on the railroad and in our neighborhood. The post doctor's services were in almost daily requisition; and as our hospital was also a tent, and many of the injured were carried there, my soul was harrowed by the cries of wounded men which could not be stifled in that clear atmosphere with nothing but canvas intervening.

One of the young officers who knew my terror on that score, delighted in giving me exaggerated accounts of their sufferings, and used to relate the most remarkable cases, which I fully believed at the time, though later his deceit and exaggeration were discovered. It seemed to me that the frontier at best was a place where suffering prevailed to a degree not commensurate with the number of inhabitants.

We were very near the " white pine region," where an immense silver mine created great excitement, the novelty of which pleased us almost as much as if we were to share in the material benefits thereof.

Mr. Boyd's promotion to a first lieutenantcy, which had been expected for many months, was

at that time received, and we hoped the railroad
would enable us to make the journey consequent upon such promotion in greater comfort
than had been possible on our previous one.
Alas! how bitterly we deplored the unalterable
fact so common in army life, that after having
endured severe hardships, and watched the advent of brighter days, as promised by the approach
of a railroad and the completion of officers'
quarters, we were compelled to leave for distant
Arizona without sharing in any of the advantages which would naturally follow.

My husband's promotion transferred him to a
company of the regiment stationed at Prescott,
Arizona Territory. We had first to reach San
Francisco, go from thence by sea to Southern
California, and then across into Arizona. One
beautiful morning, just a year from the time
of my arrival, we started for California. We
were glad to be able, instead of having to endure the discomforts of a stage-ride, to strike
the railroad twelve miles from Camp Halleck.
The road had reached that point only a few

days before, and the rails having been newly laid none but construction trains had passed over it.

We were obliged to wait for a car until the next morning, when a hospitable welcome was given us by the engineer in charge, who with his wife and family occupied the construction train, and seemed most comfortable in their movable home. They had every needful arrangement to make them so, for the cars, two in number, were roomy as possible. The first car was divided into an admirable kitchen and dining room, which were presided over by a Chinese cook ; the second into sitting and bedrooms so arranged that they were cozy and comfortable.

Our only fear was of the possibly infested atmosphere, for we were told that smallpox had broken out among the Chinese railroad employees, and was prevailing to an alarming extent. A delightful day and night were, however, passed with our new friends, who shared with us their sleeping accommodations, Mr.

Boyd rooming with the engineer and I with his wife. At nine o'clock next morning we left them, feeling very grateful for the kindness received.

Our gratitude was in no wise lessened, though our fears were increased, when the following day a telegram overtook us which stated that our engineer friend had succumbed to small-pox. He recovered from the disease perhaps sooner than we did from our panic : so great an exposure was at a most inconvenient time, for, like Joe, we had to " move on."

I was astonished to find that the car which was to take us farther West was only the caboose or freight car of an ordinary train ; and when, having climbed into the huge side opening, the steps were taken away, leaving us high and dry, the prospect was far from encouraging. There was no accommodation for comfort of any sort, and only rough benches for seats. The car, too, was filled with railroad employees, and the atmosphere soon became intolerable. The road-bed was so new and the jolting so alarming, I concluded a stage-ride would have been preferable, as we could at least have seen what was before us.

We stopped frequently, yet were so far above the ground I dared not descend, and, in fact, there was no special occasion to do so, for we rode until three the next morning before reaching a place where a mouthful of food could be obtained. Having anticipated when once on the railroad to travel so rapidly that we need make no preparations beforehand, our ride of eighteen hours in covering less than fifty miles was not only unexpected, but almost unendurable from hunger and fatigue. When at three o'clock in the morning a stopping-place was at last reached I was quite exhausted. Food and rest were found there, and best of all a civilized sleeping-car, in which we went on to Sacramento.

The journey through Nevada seemed incredibly swift. As we crossed the Sierra Nevada mountains and passed through twenty-five miles of snow-sheds, which cut off the view just as one began to enjoy it, I felt almost glad to have taken what had become so completely a memory of the past — a stage-ride over those grand old mountains.

It was wonderful to observe the marked difference in vegetation between Nevada and California. Just as soon as we reached the Pacific coast exquisite green verdure contrasted so favorably with Nevada's arid desolation as to cause one to feel as if in a veritable " land of promise." The refreshment to our weary eyes after a year of absence from such scenery was a source of the greatest imaginable pleasure. Then to cover in a few short hours the same distance which had previously required five weary days and nights was not the least of our many causes for gratitude. When Sacramento was reached, the exquisite beauty of the country was so great we felt that all the encomiums California had ever received were fully warranted.

The next day we arrived in San Francisco, and once more felt civilized.

CHAPTER IV.

MY husband's first duty was to report to the commanding general, who gave him permission to remain there for two months, promising to place him on duty in order that he might receive full pay and allowances. That seemed a very great boon until we found the duty consisted in Mr. Boyd's being ordered five hundred miles away to inspect some horses, which left me utterly lonely in a strange city.

The place to which he was sent could be reached only by water, and the steamers sailed weekly both going and returning, so I felt particularly forlorn, knowing he could not be back for at least ten days. When the first return steamer reached San Francisco without him I was in despair, and indeed with reason. I had already found the tender mercy of a boardinghouse keeper to be all it is generally repre-sented.

That night our little daughter was born, and a facetious friend telegraphed to my husband: "Mother and child are doing well," thus leaving the sex to be conjectured, which caused bets to be made by such officers as were always glad of an excuse to bet on any chance.

But, indeed, "mother and child" were not doing well. A veritable Sairy Gamp had taken possession of both: my own sufferings were almost intolerable, while I felt sure the poor little baby was being continually dosed. The nurse weighed nearly three hundred pounds, and at night when she lay down beside me her enormous weight made such an inclined plane of the bed that I could not keep from rolling against her; and she snored so loudly that not only was it impossible for me to sleep, but for any one else on the same floor. The sounds were not at all sedative in their effects, and I spent the nights praying for morning.

My baby, too, was so restless that her position had to be frequently changed; and when the nurse was awakened she treated me exactly as if I were a naughty child, and so completely cowed me by her roughness that I dared offer no remonstrance, but simply endured.

Matters went on thus for several days until some of the kind ladies in the house interfered; but not before I had been left entirely alone the night our little one was a week old, and was found unconscious with baby screaming so loudly that every one in the house was aroused.

The good old days are not so much to be deplored when we consider that the nurse was a fair specimen of her class, and had no hesitancy in asking forty dollars a week for the services she rendered. Now that trained nurses are to be found everywhere, such creatures are unknown. Instances of her cruel conduct might be multiplied, but it is unnecessary.

As usual I was tormented by fears on the score of expense, as all supplies were most exorbitant in price. The increase in rank had added only one hundred dollars a year to my husband's pay, and the land of fruitful abundance in which we then were was almost as costly, so far as living expenses were concerned, as the frontier, and under the circumstances far more so.

After two steamers had arrived without bringing Mr. Boyd, I grew so restless under the care of such a nurse that the determination to discharge her was formed; yet sufficient courage to do so was not summoned until after the arrival of my husband, five days before our baby was three weeks old.

We then essayed to minister to baby's wants ourselves, and some of the attempts were ludicrous. Having seen the nurse give the child paregoric, once, when she cried desperately, I poured out a teaspoonful, and while my husband held baby, tried to make her swallow it. Had not the drug in its raw strength nearly strangled her, we would, undoubtedly, have murdered our dear little infant.

That was not the only experiment we tried, and looking back I pity the poor child with all

my heart. Our anxiety to improve her appearance was so great that whatever we were ad-
vised to do was attempted. I cut off baby's
eyelashes one day to make them grow thicker;
and when she was a little older, while we were
in Arizona, I found her father pressing that
dear little nose between the prongs of a clothes-
pin to better its shape. She resented such
treatment, and her cries filled me with indignation, for at least my experiments had all been
painless.

The day after Mr. Boyd's return, notwithstanding the commanding general's promise
that we should remain in San Francisco until
May, orders were received to proceed immediately to Arizona. It never occurred to my husband that he should dispute the order, nor to
me that I could remain for a time in California.

After a couple of days spent in purchasing
needful supplies and hunting the city over for
a servant, we took steamer for Wilmington in
Southern California. The trip occupied two
days, and as we kept very near the coast,

choppy seas made me extremely seasick and miserable. I was so thin and pale as to excite the sympathies of all who saw me. The doctor had said that the change would benefit me. while, perhaps, I could not improve if left in California. His prediction might have proved true had not the journey been so fearfully hard. Baby was exactly three weeks old the day we reached Los Angeles, from which place we were to start on our long interior ride.

Nothing can be more beautiful than were the surroundings of that town. As we drove in from Wilmington the air was odorous with the perfume of orange blossoms; and trees, heavy with their loads of ripening fruits of different kinds, overshadowed our road. I have never cared for oranges since eating those brought me still clinging to their branches: no packed fruit can compare with such in flavor and lusciousness.

Having been housed so long I enjoyed to the full the flowers that bloomed on all sides, making a perfect paradise of the spot. My recollections of California, for I have never seen it since, are most delightful, and I deem any one fortunate who has a settled home there.

That part of Southern California is particularly favored, and my recollections of the five days consumed in traveling toward the East are among the pleasantest of my life. We stopped every night at some ranch, where the occupants not only received us kindly, but where our eyes could feast on glorious scenery, which combined with the liberal creature comforts that were enjoyed, left little to be wished for.

I longed to remain in Los Angeles; but we were obliged to hurry on in compliance with military orders, and also for another reason. An entire day spent in San Francisco hunting for a servant had only resulted in procuring a Chinese boy twelve years old. No woman could be induced to go to Arizona. First, because no church was there. Second, and mainly, because many Indians were.

Even the mercenary Chinese had never dreamed of passing into so dangerous a region;

and when on reaching Los Angeles my little servant naturally exchanged confidences with those employed in the hotel, such a tale of horrors — principally in the shape of Indian cruelties — was told the boy, that he was terrified beyond belief, and fairly shook with anguish and fear when informed that he must accompany us. Evidently believing that his long queue would prove an additional inducement for the Indians to scalp him, he was determined to escape at all hazards. Our little servant could be kept from running away only by locking him up; he was not released until we were ready to step into the wagon, and a more woebegone face I have never seen.

It is to this day an historical fact, both in Arizona and New Mexico, that we took the first Chinaman into those States which now swarm with them, and where only recently they were boycotted.

For some reason unknown to us, we were refused proper transportation — an ambulance and four mules with driver. A small, two-seated vehicle and span of horses had instead been provided, which when loaded with our most needed articles presented a strange appearance. A mattress and blankets were strapped on the back, and over those a chair. The inside was simply crowded with an array of articles demanded by our long journey. We had not only all necessary clothing, but as much food in a condensed shape as could be taken; there was no room for luxuries. Our first care was to be well armed, as we were going among hostile Indians, a fact I could scarcely realize; therefore our vehicle held, in addition to all else, a gun, two pistols, and strapped overhead my husband's two sabers, which he required when on duty.

Some premonition, which perhaps was the result of past experience, made me careful to select all we might need for future as well as present use in the way of clothing. It proved a wise precaution, for the remainder of our baggage, including all household goods, which we had left in the hands of freighters, was seized for their debts on the borders of California, and not permitted to cross into Arizona until means to liquidate the men's obligations had been found. It took just six months to do that, during which time we waited for our property.

With my usual docility in accepting advice concerning baby, I had followed the suggestion of an army paymaster's wife, who considered a champagne basket the proper receptacle for an infant when traveling. Never was advice given which proved more useful or beneficial. If with all the other hardships of that journey I had been compelled to hold baby day after day, not only would I have been far more fatigued, but she far less comfortable. Cradled in that basket, the motion of our carriage acted as a perpetual lullaby, and the little one slept soundly all the time, waking only when progress ceased. The basket was tightly strapped to the front seat beside my husband, who drove, while I sat on the back one with our little Chinaman.

CHAPTER V.

THE time-honored "babes in the woods" could not have started on their pilgrimage with more childlike simplicity than did my husband and myself. The first five days, through the most beautiful country imaginable, were like a pleasure trip, and little prepared us for the hardships which followed. The roads were good, the scenery superb, and each night we were most hospitably entertained by some kind family.

Besides good food and comfortable beds, considerable advice as to the treatment of baby was thrown in gratuitously. It seemed all the more necessary just then, for although during the entire trip our little one slept sweetly throughout the day, no doubt lulled to rest by the motion of the vehicle, when night came she was tortured by that baby's enemy — colic. As a cure, we kept adding to her coverings, until no one could have dreamed that the tightly strapped and blanketed basket contained a human being. Many were the comments of surprise when the child was exhumed from her manifold wrappings. If the custom of traveling by carriage long distances was not almost obsolete, I should advise all young mothers to try the basket plan. Not only was baby perfectly comfortable, but the saving of my strength was great, and that alone enabled me to survive the journey.

We passed the celebrated Cocomungo Ranch, with its beautiful vineyards and delicious wines, and many other spots, then unoccupied lands, which have since become populous towns. On the fifth day Camp Cady, where we expected to take final leave of civilization and enter the California desert, was reached. The camp was garrisoned by a detachment of only twenty men, and but two could be spared as an escort for us. Even then the wife of the officer in charge demurred, saying:

"Suppose the Indians should attack us? What could we do with only eighteen men?"

When during subsequent weeks I fully realized the dangers we were encountering, her remark was frequently recalled. Certainly two men were not sufficient to protect us from Indians.

Immediately after leaving Camp Cady we descended into a small cañon, and on emerging therefrom found ourselves dragging through deep sand, which continued for miles and was wearisome in the extreme. Our horses plodded along, and the monotony of desert travel was thoroughly established. Only eighteen miles were covered that day, yet it took ten hours, as we dared not urge the horses through such deep sand.

Our first encampment was a memorable one. Like all desert travelers, we did not stop on account of having reached an oasis, but simply because our horses could go no farther. I wondered then, as on our previous journey, why the particular spot at which we stopped had been selected. It always seemed to me that we might have gone on; but that was not a common-sense view — merely an eager desire to hasten toward home.

I never knew why we had no tent of any kind, not even the tiny shelter tent with which every soldier is supposed to be provided on all journeys; I do, however, know that we had not a stitch of canvas of any sort, and that baby was awakened every morning by the glaring sun shining full in her face. As the sun on the desert sand is reflective, we soon learned to dread it extremely.

I wish it were possible to impress others with the sensation those camps invariably produced upon me! Usually occupying as a spectator a passive position, I sat apart and watched the blazing fire and the figures of the men sharply defined against its light as they prepared supper, and then, peering into the unfathomable distance of loneliness beyond and on all sides, I indulged in all kinds of visions, none of which were calculated to make me especially happy.

That night, however, the men who accompanied us pretended to be unequal to the task of making ready our slight repast, and I essayed for the first time in my life, and under the greatest disadvantages, to cook an entire meal. A strong wind was blowing, which drove the smoke in my face and eyes. The more I tried to avoid this, the more it seemed to torture me; while my utter lack of knowledge in all culinary matters, especially when prosecuted under such circumstances, was very trying. Baby added to my misery by screaming with pain from her usual attack of colic.

Want of space in our little wagon had compelled us to forego all but the actual necessaries of life; and thus our bill of fare was limited to bacon, hard tack, and a small supply of eggs, which, with coffee, was our only food during that desert travel of five days. I learned to grill bacon and make excellent coffee, but never to enjoy cooking over a camp-fire.

Bright and early, awakened by the sun shining full in our faces, we started on our seventh day's journey, which proved almost exactly like our sixth, yet closed with a tragic incident. The horses were our pride and glory — they were not only beautiful, but strong and useful. Watching them as they carried us along so swiftly and safely during the first five days had been a real pleasure, and we had become attached to the faithful animals.

On reaching Soda Lake at the end of our seventh day's journey, and second after leaving Camp Cady, we were not a little dismayed to find that the horses were suffering quite severely from the effects of their hard two days' pull through the deep sand. On being unharnessed, one immediately plunged into the lake, and in spite of all efforts remained there. The result may be conjectured. In his heated and exhausted condition he foundered, and to our great sorrow had to be shot.

That was a serious hindrance to our progress ; but, fortunately, we had with us a pack-mule laden with grain for the horses. Needless to state he was relieved of his load, much of which we left by the roadside; the remainder, necessary for the animals' sustenance, was placed in our wagon, which rendered us still more uncomfortable. It would be difficult to tell what we did with our feet, for not an inch of space on the bottom of the wagon was unoccupied.

We left Soda Lake with joy, as its alkaline properties rendered the water useless for all ordinary purposes, and a better supply was longed for. During that entire desert journey, until the Colorado River was reached, we had not a drop of water that could quench thirst. Both men and animals were to be pitied.

Our eighth day was dreadful in its manner of progress. The pack-mule, quite unaccustomed to harness, had no idea of bearing his share of the burden, while our beautiful little mare chafed in the company of such an ungainly creature, and seemed so desirous to be rid of him that she did all the pulling. For days our minds were occupied with the problem of how to restrain her and urge on the mule. Every effort to accomplish this only made mat-

ters worse, for it invariably resulted in the latter breaking into a clumsy, lumbering gallop
that was very ludicrous.

At length we left the deep sand and traveled
over the most level country imaginable. It
proved, however, even more dreary, for the
ground was white as snow with alkaline de-
posits. As far as the eye could reach, only an
endless, white, barren plain, unrelieved by even
a scrub bush, was visible. In all my frontier
life and travel I never saw anything so utterly
desolate as was that desert.

We found, after the first day of unmatched
steeds, that our little mare must be favored or
she too would die. It was therefore decided to
travel mainly at night. The ground was so
hard and white that the sun's reflection was
most dazzling. When, on the ninth day, we
encamped with only our wagon to shade us
from its intense rays, I would have given almost
anything for the shelter a strip of canvas would
have afforded. Long before noon, and long
after, the pitiless sun poured down upon us,

until hands and faces were blistered; even poor little baby had to be smeared with glycerine as a preventive.

In that manner we traveled for two days over the desert; and although the sun's heat was almost unendurable, yet our only safety lay in so doing.

We started about sundown on the ninth night, and reaching an old disused house about midnight, prepared to camp. I had been so tortured for several days and nights by the absence of all shelter, that my husband readily complied with the request to place our mattress inside those old walls. The roof had long before disappeared: but it seemed good to be once more in any sort of inclosure, and I lay down very composedly. My sleep was, however, soon disturbed by the strangest sounds. I awakened to find that a veritable carnival was being held by insects, and the uncertainty concerning their species was anything but agreeable. Every imaginable noise could be detected. I bore it silently as long as possible, until confident I heard rattlesnakes, when in great fear I hugged my baby closer, expecting our last moments had come, yet hoping to shield her from their fangs.

Such a night of wretchedness I hope never again to experience. All kinds of horrible sounds terrified me to such an extent that a firm resolve was formed never to pass another night in a place of whose inhabitants I was unaware. I am confident that every sort of vermin infested that old ruined house, and our subsequent perils with visible foes gave me far less anxiety.

Having learned to dread being a source of extra trouble to Mr. Boyd on a journey which taxed every energy of his mind and body, I always endured everything quietly as long as possible. That alone enabled me to go through such a night of agony — interminable it seemed at the time, but in reality only a few hours, for dawn soon came.

Midday again found us on our way; and when we began to descend into the Colorado basin, and caught sight of Fort Mojave's adobe walls and the muddy banks of the river, we felt as if the end of a hard journey had at last been reached, and rejoiced exceedingly to see friendly faces and receive a hearty welcome. Knowing that each day's travel was bringing us nearer home, we gladly crossed the river and shook the dust of California from our feet.

CHAPTER VI.

FORT. MOJAVE, at that time a mere collection of adobe buildings with no special pretensions to comfort, stood on the eastern bank of the Colorado River. It seemed to me, except for the extreme heat which made it an uncomfortable sleeping-place, a very haven of rest. The muddy river sluggishly wound its way to the gulf many miles below, and nine months of the year the temperature of every place on its banks was torrid. Fort Yuma, at its mouth, was noted for being a veritable Tophet.

A yarn illustrative of the general opinion of its climate is told of a soldier who ventured out in the middle of a July day, and never returned. Diligent search served only to discover a huge grease-spot and pile of bones on the parade ground.

Another tradition, very hackneyed to army ears, is that of a soldier famous for his wickedness, who, having died, reappeared, and was seen hunting for his blankets; the inference being that the warm place to which he had been assigned was not hot enough for one accustomed to Fort Yuma's climate.

All ladies who have lived there supplement these ridiculous tales with more credible ones. It is quite true that eggs, if not gathered as soon as laid, were sure to be roasted if the sun shone on them. It is also a fact that those who had leisure to do so spent the greater part of their time in the bath, and Indians would remain in the stream for hours at a time, their heads covered with mud as a protection from the sun's rays.

I soon realized that not being obliged to remain in so warm a climate was a favor, and rejoiced greatly when once more fairly *en route*, although the two days had been very pleasantly passed. We were furnished with a pair of mules, so our poor little mare could be led the remainder of the way, and we had as escort two men who were sent into Arizona with the weekly mails.

Our first day's travel was pleasant; but when night came on we were alarmed at the number of signal fires on all sides, which indicated the near presence of hostile Indians. I shall never forget the shock experienced when I first realized that we were in danger from such a source. The past year had so accustomed me to Indians, that it seemed as if all tribes were harmless; yet the constant wariness of our escort soon convinced me of the contrary.

The part of Arizona through which we were then passing was such an agreeable contrast to our weary desert journey that I thoroughly enjoyed the beautiful pine lands; and the change, as we ascended daily into more mountainous regions, was delightful. Our second day from Fort Mojave, and the twelfth of that long journey, however, considerably dampened my ardor.

The road had been rough from the start, but nothing to be compared with what we then experienced. After a tedious ascent a long hill was reached, seemingly miles in length, and which must be descended amid boulders strewn all over the road. I was compelled to walk, with baby in my arms, picking my way as best I could from one rock to another. The time occupied in making the descent was three hours. My fatigue can hardly be imagined.

The wagon wheels were lashed together by ropes, which were held by men on either side; and even then the vehicle fairly bounded onward, each leap almost wrenching it asunder. I expected every moment to see it lying in ruins. That such was not its fate was entirely due to the care Mr. Boyd and the men took in guiding it safely between and over the boulders.

No hill I have ever since seen was like that, and no words are adequate to give any idea of its horrors. I felt every moment as if a single mis-step would launch my infant and self into eternity, and wondered if I could survive the fatigue, even if successful in placing my feet carefully enough to escape the greater danger. When finally our little company at the foot of the hill was reached, I sank, completely exhausted. Many days passed before I could step without feeling the effects of that terrible scramble in mid-air.

We had hoped to reach our destination in four days after leaving Fort Mojave; but each day seemed longer than its predecessor, especially as dangers increased. Our second night was spent in a military camp, and a detachment of troops guarded the highway. I could no longer doubt the necessity of exercising constant vigilance against hostile foes.

Every animal in the temporary stables had been maimed in some manner by Indians, who would steal in under cover of darkness and shoot whatever living thing they saw. The men were always in peril, even in their tents; and the officer in charge did not lessen in any degree my uneasiness when he showed me how his tent had been riddled in many places by bullets. He was then recovering from the effects of a wound received while pursuing Indians.

We had breakfasted, and were about ready to start next morning, when our attention was called to Indians' footprints all over the garden-spot which the troops had prepared for their hoped for supply of vegetables. Alas for the poor people who in those days thought to make fortunes out West! No amount of energy, perseverance, or endurance, to say nothing of hardships bravely borne, could ward off the cruel Indians.

Although it may be justly said that our dealings with the red men were the primary cause of all the suffering, yet could the hundreds of settlers who lost their lives while endeavoring to make homes for themselves in the West be avenged, not an Indian would be left to tell the tale. My heart was wrung during those travels, when, every hour of the day, we passed a pile of stones that marked a grave. Arizona seemed to me a very burying-ground — a huge cemetery — for men and women killed by Indians.

In after-years I agreed perfectly with the
common army belief that attempting to settle a
ranch in either Arizona or New Mexico was
simply courting an inevitable fate — death at
the hands of ruthless Indians. History was
ever new in those regions, and kept ever repeat-
ing itself. I frequently heard it said, referring
to a comparatively recent settler:

"Well, his time will surely come."

Whenever a ranch was in an exceptionally
isolated region, the sequel would be accelerated.
Indian horrors were every-day occurrences; and
yet I never grew accustomed to them. Long
residence among those much-abused frontiersmen taught me to feel that the early martyrs
suffered little in comparison with the constant
peril in which they lived.

But to return to our journey and its growing
dangers. A number of soldiers escorted us
through a perilous cañon outside of the little
detachment post, where, at ten o'clock, our
officer friend reluctantly bade us adieu, saying
we were in great danger. Could his post have

been left with safety, he would willingly have escorted us farther.

We rode on, feeling indeed very anxious, and soon met a Major of the Eighth Cavalry, who with an escort of sixteen men had been peppered by Indians' bullets in a cañon through which we must pass the same day. As the escort of two men with which we left Camp Cady had not been augmented, our feelings may be imagined. There was no alternative; go on we must.

I now see that we were then too young and inexperienced to realize the dangers of our terrible position. It was, however, soon understood, and before entering the cañon at six o'clock that evening all warlike preparations possible under the circumstances had been made. A civilian had joined our party at Fort Mojave, and thus there were three outriders. The two sabres in our wagon overhead we took down and unsheathed, so that, when thrust out on either side, there seemed to be four weapons — at least we hoped the Indians would think so,

and unless they came very close, the dim light
would favor our deception. The gun was
placed so it could be used at a moment's notice.
I held one pistol, and Mr. Boyd the other. The
soldiers, with their bayonets bristling, looked as
warlike as possible ; and altogether we relied
upon what eventually saved our lives — an
appearance of strength which we in nowise
possessed.

We had been told that the Indians, at least
in that region, never attacked unless confident
of victory; and we knew that unless they were
directly beside us, the appearance our wagon
presented, so covered they could not see its interior, and seemingly full of weapons, would
indicate a well-armed party of men. Instead,
there was one man, handicapped by the care
of his team and the helpless nature of his
charges — a feeble woman, an infant, and a
diminutive heathen, who on perceiving the active preparations being made for resisting what
he had so feared, became literally green with
terror and altogether useless.

The cañon was so precipitous on both sides that we seemed to be traveling between two high walls. The rocks were of that treacherous gray against which I had been told an Indian could so effectually conceal himself as to seem but a part of them. The entire region was weird and awful. The sides of the cañon towered far above us to almost unseen heights, and as we slowly drove onward, our hearts quivered with excitement and fear at the probability of an attack.

We had proceeded some little distance and were feeling considerably relieved, when suddenly a fearful Indian war-whoop arose. It was so abrupt, and seemed such a natural outcome of our fears, that only for repeated repetitions I could have believed it imaginary. Others, however, quickly followed, so no doubt could be entertained of their reality. I had only sufficient consciousness to wonder when we should die, and how. I glanced involuntarily at our Chinese servant, who was crouched in one corner of the wagon in a most pitiable heap, and then at our poor little baby, bundled in many wraps and sleeping in her basket. All were silent. No word was uttered, and no sound heard but the lashing of the whip that urged forward our mules. Although they fairly leaped onward, yet we seemed to crawl. Cruel death was momentarily expected.

At last, and it seemed ages, we were out of the cañon and on open ground. Even then no time was lost. The mules were still hurried on. I have often thought that, like Tennyson's brook, we might have "gone on forever" had not a large party of freighters soon been reached, who were camping in front of a blazing wood fire. Their presence gave us that sense of companionship and security so sorely needed. We joined them; and while I sat in the blaze of their fire, Mr. Boyd recounted our perilous ride. The conclusion was reached that we had been spared only because apparently so well prepared to resist attack. Any doubts which might have been entertained concerning the presence of foes in the cañon were dispelled by what followed.

I crawled that night under a wagon, for my nerves were too shattered to sleep without some kind of shelter if it could be procured, and my last waking thought was that our companions for the night would have to pass next morning through the same dangerous cañon, their destination being California. They started first, and one of the superintendents — there were two in the party — foolishly disregarded our warning and lagged behind. His mangled body was afterwards found horribly mutilated on the very spot where we had heard the Indians' fearful yells.

It was a well-known fact that the savages would lurk for days in one place, and if disappointed by any party being too numerous or well armed, would invariably later on destroy some careless straggler. The freighters, having escaped such dangers again and again, would frequently become reckless, when they were almost sure to finally fall victims to their lack of caution.

CHAPTER VII.

ONLY two days were left in which to reach our destination. The remainder of the road was level, and no further danger from Indians need be apprehended. Our next encampment was at Willow Grove, a lovely wooded spot where some of our own troops were stationed, and but a short distance from what we supposed was to be our home, at least for a time.

At last Prescott, then a mining-town, was gained. Everything seemed delightful. Situated among the hills, surrounded by trees, and with a most enjoyable climate, never very hot or very cold, but bracing at all seasons, it would indeed prove a desirable home to wanderers like ourselves, and I fondly hoped we might remain there.

We were warmly welcomed at the garrison,

which was situated half a mile from town. There were but three houses in the post, and all occupied. The houses contained only three rooms each, and one of the officers kindly relinquished his room in my favor. The ladies were very hospitable in providing me with nourishing food, of which I was in great need.

Our dismay on learning that Mr. Boyd must leave the next day to join his company, which had been sent eighty miles distant to a post called Camp Date Creek, may be imagined. The movement was considered only temporary, as the troop was permanently stationed at Prescott; so, supposing that my husband might return almost immediately, it was decided that I should remain there.

All would have gone well had there been suitable accommodations; but no sooner had Mr. Boyd left than the inspector-general, accompanied by several other officers, arrived, and their baggage was placed in the room I was occupying. There was no alternative but for me to move into the adjoining room, an old, deserted kitchen, which had for years past been the receptacle of miscellaneous *débris.*

My bed had to be made on the floor between two windows, whose panes of glass were either cracked or broken. An old stove, utterly useless, occupied the hearth. As the nights and mornings were very cold I tried to build a fire; but the smoke, instead of ascending, poured into the room in volumes, and compelled me to abandon the task as hopeless. I suffered far more from the cold there than I had while on the march, and longed for a camp-fire.

The kitchen was a perfect curiosity shop. Garments of every imaginable kind, when no longer of use to their owners, had evidently been left there. An " old clothes man " would have rejoiced at the wealth of rubbish. I counted twenty pairs of boots and shoes, and there were quite as many hats, coats, and nether garments. The corners of that room were to be avoided as one would avoid the plague. My chair, which had been brought from California, was planted in the only clean spot — the floor's immediate center.

I tried to imagine myself camping out, but my surroundings were far less agreeable than they would have been in that case, and whichever way my eyes turned, they met unsightly objects. No one seemed to consider the situation unpleasant, so I simply resigned myself to the inevitable.

After I had been living in that way for ten days, the post surgeon came in and said:

" Mrs. Boyd, I have observed your disagreeable plight if no one else has, and am exceedingly sorry. I am ordered to Camp Date Creek, and if you would like will escort you."

No farther words were needed. I was ready to leave immediately ; and when told of the disagreeables that would be encountered simply laughed, I was so tired of homelessness.

Prescott was in such a healthy location as to be a very desirable station, while Camp Date Creek was low and malarious. The post statistics showed that eighty per cent of the men were then suffering from fever. The extreme heat and numerous supply of vermin were also enlarged upon; but nothing daunted me, and I went on my way rejoicing.

The journey was indeed very trying. The road was principally a lava bed, and we were fearfully jolted. I disliked making trouble, and remember riding for miles, holding on to the basket in which baby was lying, which had been placed on the bottom of the vehicle at my feet. To prevent the basket — precious contents and all — from slipping out under the front seat, I was obliged to cling tightly to it, and at the same time firmly brace myself in order to keep from being tossed about.

However, everything must have an end — even such a journey. I was inexpressibly glad to find a house once more over my head, and to receive my husband's hearty welcome.

Army life is uncertain in the extreme, and our detail proved no exception to the rule. The troop was sent to Camp Date Creek for a month, but it remained a year, until the regiment left Arizona. The consolidation of regiments was at that time being effected.

The infantry had been reduced from forty to twenty-five regiments, which necessitated many moves, and was the occasion for the detention there of some troops until more infantry arrived.

It was indeed a desolate and undesirable locality. The country was ugly, flat, and inexpressibly dreary. The section stretching in front of our camp was called "bad lands" (*mala pice*). The only pretty spot at all near was a slow, sluggish stream some miles away, where no one dared remain long for fear of malaria.

Our only associate was the doctor, and subsequently, when a company of infantry arrived, two officers ; but for at least six months of that year I was the only woman within at least fifty miles. I found, too, that housekeeping was a burden ; for in all the travel from north to south, and the reverse, through Arizona, every one stopped *en route*. Before we left I felt competent to keep a hotel if experience was any education in the art. Even stage passengers had frequently to be cared for, as in that region it would have been cruel, when delays occurred, to have permitted them to have gone farther without food.

As usual, I had the help of a soldier; but unfortunately one who, when he found that too much was likely to be required of him, took refuge in intoxication; then the entire burden fell upon me. Our little Chinese boy proved a treasure. He could wash and iron capitally, excepting my husband's shirts and the baby's clothes, the ironing of both of which came upon me.

That year of my life was, in spite of many hardships, a very happy one. I have often since wondered how it could have been so, for surely no one ever lived more queerly. The houses were built of mud-brick (adobe), which was not, as is usual, plastered either inside or out. Being left unfinished they soon began to crumble in the dry atmosphere, and large holes or openings formed, in which vermin, especially centipeds, found hiding-places. The latter were so plentiful that I have frequently counted a dozen or more crawling in and out of the interstices. Scorpions and rattlesnakes also took up their abode with us, and one snake of a more harmless nature used almost daily to thrust his head through a hole in the floor. Altogether we had plenty of such visitors.

In faithfully recording my experiences, honesty compels me to state that although I have encountered almost every species of noxious and deadly vermin, from the ubiquitous rattlesnake to the deadly vinageroon, my real trials have arisen from the simpler sorts, such as wasps, gnats, fleas, flies, and mosquitoes, which, everywhere prolific, are doubly so on the frontier. I think a kind Providence must have watched over our encounters with deadly reptiles, though nothing could save us from ordinary pests.

Perhaps the most trying of all my experiences was when we made our camp after dark. On those occasions we would be almost certain either to find that our tents had been erected close beside a bed of cacti, to fall into whenever we moved, or over an ant-heap of such dimensions that cannot be conceived of by any one in the East. The busy population of one of those ant-hills was among the millions; and evidently each inhabitant felt called upon to resent our intrusion, for soon we would be literally covered with the stinging pests. When our little ones were the victims, as often happened, we longed to live in a land where such creatures were unknown.

But to return to a description of our home. The house consisted of one long room, with a door at either end, and two windows on each side. The room was sufficiently large to enable us to divide it by a canvas curtain, and thus have a sitting-room and bedroom. We felt very happy on account of having a floor other than the ground, though it consisted only of broad, rough, unplaned planks, which had shrunk so that the spaces between them were at least two inches in width, and proved a trap for every little article that fell upon the floor.

The brown, rough adobe walls were very uninviting, and centipeds were so numerous I never dared place our bed within at least two feet of them. The adjoining house, which was vacant, I used for a dining-room. Our kitchen stood as far away in another direction, so I seemed to daily walk miles in the simple routine of housekeeping duties.

The country was very desolate, and the dismal cry of the coyotes at night anything but enlivening. Those animals became so bold as actually to approach our door, and one night carried off a box of shoe-blacking. They evidently did not care for that kind of relish, as it was discovered next day a short distance from the house.

We killed so many snakes that I made a collection of rattles. One of the tales told about me was that a box of them sent to New York was labelled "Rattlesnakes' Rattles! Poison!" Of course that was not true; but our lives were so monotonous we enjoyed any joke on each other.

I thought the last would never have been heard of my early pronunciation of "Fort Mojave," which it is probably needless to state was exactly in English accord with its spelling. Probably had I known the word was Spanish, not understanding the language, my pronunciation would have been the same.

I was always delighted when ladies passed through the post, and invariably begged them to remain as long as possible. One lovely woman, whose husband had been ordered from Southern to Northern Arizona, only to find on reaching there that his station was to be but twenty miles from the place he had just left, gladdened me twice by her presence. When I expressed regret because she was obliged to traverse the same road again during such extremely warm weather, her assurance that she did not in the least mind it, surprised and relieved me.

I found Arizona even worse than Nevada, so far as supplies were concerned. We could seldom obtain luxuries of any kind, and when procurable they were exorbitant in price. Eggs cost two dollars and fifty cents a dozen; butter the same per pound; chickens two dollars and fifty cents apiece; potatoes, twenty cents per pound; kerosene oil, five dollars a gallon, and I was told it had been as high as fourteen dollars. Fortunately we could buy candles at government rates.

We were often at our wit's ends to supply food for guests. I had five bantam chickens, that each laid an egg daily for some time, which we considered great cause for thankfulness. I actually learned to concoct dainties without many of the ingredients usually supposed necessary, and they were declared very good.

Finally, after having been at Camp Date Creek some months, another lady joined us, at which I rejoiced exceedingly. She proved a very great acquisition to our army circle.

Our mail was due once a week, but became very uncertain on account of the Indians. Mr. Boyd was twice awakened late at night by sentries, who reported the return of one man very badly wounded, and that the other had been left dead, and the mail scattered all over the country. Whenever the drums beat over the remains of any young man, thoughts of his absent friends always came to me. Our miserable little cemetery, out on that lonely plain, had not one grave whose quiet occupant was more than twenty-three·years of age, and none had died a natural death.

My husband was the busiest man imaginable. He had not only to command his company, but was also in charge of all stores and buildings. The quartermaster's storehouse was a long distance off, and Mr. Boyd was there all day long. I used to be in continual fear lest Indians should attack him. No greater diligence could have been displayed by any one, and no one could have worked more conscientiously or faithfully than he did all through life.

We feared to ride over the country on account of the Indians, and therefore had less amusement and recreation than while in Nevada, yet contentment shed its blessed rays about us. I was always joyful, and ceased to wish that the hardships we were enduring might be exchanged for even attic life if in New York. My regret on learning that we were to leave for New Mexico was keen, although aware better quarters were awaiting us. But I had grown to love my Arizona home, if the walls were only rough adobe ones. In just nine months from the time of my arrival at Date Creek, and in midwinter, we left for our new destination. It was with vexation of spirit that I again took up the march.

CHAPTER VIII.

As an illustration of the many delays consequent upon frontier travel may be mentioned
the receipt, just before leaving for New Mexico,
of a box that had been fourteen months *en
route*, though sent by express from New York.
To recount the mishaps which had befallen it
would be tiresome ; yet that was but one of
many similar experiences.

I had ordered the box in December, while at
Camp Halleck, fully expecting it would reach
San Francisco by the time we did.   The contents were very valuable, and included an army
overcoat intended as a surprise for my husband,
together with many other useful and needed
additions to our wardrobe.

It was shipped by my brother, who mailed
at the same time two bills of lading.   The

box arrived safely by sea, but the mail, which was sent overland, was snowbound on the Union Pacific, and consequently our letters were delayed. Knowing my brother's habitual promptness, I haunted the express office in San Francisco, only to be told again and again that no such box was there. We therefore started for Arizona without it. On our arrival, letters and the two bills of lading were awaiting us. The box had been in San Francisco all the time.

One of the bills was intrusted to an officer going there, who promised to attend to the matter, but he never troubled himself about it. After months had elapsed we begged another officer to hunt up the box, which he not only did, but kindly brought it to us, after its arrival had been vainly expected for fourteen months. The strangest part of the whole affair, to my unworldly mind, was that the first officer was under great obligations to us, while the one who really obtained the box was almost a stranger.

The present may not seem a fitting occasion

to moralize; but as this is a true account of my army life and experience, I desire to state that my reward for undue exertions on any one's behalf was usually the basest ingratitude. Of course this is only in accordance with all the time-honored maxims of wiser people than myself, but the personal experience was none the less unpleasant.

The officer to whom I refer as having been under obligations, had brought a sick wife and child to the post for a temporary sojourn, but the illness of his wife was so prolonged I was completely worn out nursing her. As an addition to my troubles a second child appeared upon the scene, which I was not only compelled to care for, but supply with a wardrobe, in order that they might leave for California in a month's time. I was ill in bed, the result of overwork, for weeks after they left, yet never have received a line from them.

My long experience on the frontier plainly demonstrated that the absence of civilization and all its appliances compelled any one with a

sympathetic heart to learn all branches of nursing. Before having been married ten years I
had acted as midwife at least that number of
times, and, far sadder, had prepared sweet and
beautiful women for their last resting-places.

Few who have seen delicately nurtured city
girls marry so gladly the men of their choice,
have any idea of what they must endure in
army life. The utter absence of so much that
is considered indispensable in ordinary homes,
added to the constant possibility of a move at
the most infelicitous moment, causes anxiety
and restlessness which have no adequate com-
pensations in either the emoluments or glory
that can be gained in the service. Children
always enjoy frontier travel, but anxiety falls
to the lot of mothers.

In one march of our regiment from New
Mexico to Texas, nine children were born *en
route*. In those instances which came under
my observation, both mothers and babies were
on the second day bundled into ambulances and
marched onward. In my opinion the natural

desire of army officers' wives to be with their husbands has cost the sacrifice of many precious lives; while those who survive the hardships have bitter sufferings to contend with in after years of chronic illness.

It is notorious that no provision is made for women in the army. Many indignation meetings were held at which we discussed the matter, and rebelled at being considered mere camp followers. It is a recognized fact that woman's presence — as wife — alone prevents demoralization, and army officers are always encouraged to marry for that reason.

While at Camp Date Creek we formed several pleasant friendships, and it is a matter of regret that in the years which have since elapsed I have never met any of the ladies. Through the resignation of our company captain and promotion of the senior lieutenant, an addition was made to our circle of a brave, true soldier — a man appointed from the ranks — who by his nobility of character graced the higher position.

Consolidation at that time weeded out all

worthless men. If an officer's reputation was aspersed, the charges were investigated, and if proved, the chances of retaining his commission were very slight.

A second lieutenant of our troop was a scamp. He victimized me before receiving his *congé*. I had supposed the mere title, " officer of the army," to be synonymous with honesty, so intrusted to him the hoardings of many months with which I had designed to purchase a pipe, and present to my husband. The amount, seventy-five dollars, was large to me, and evidently to him also, for I never saw the money again, nor the pipe it was to buy. Neither did the lieutenant return, for he was dismissed the service, or rather dropped for incompetency.

Mr. Boyd had his pipe after all; for not discouraged by my loss I began to save again, and although funds accumulated slowly, and a year passed before the requisite amount was laid by, the pipe remains to this day a memento of my early extravagance.

We had no outside society at Date Creek

except a few rough frontiersmen, who not only dared the danger from Indians, but also that of the low, malarious atmosphere, for the sake of raising vegetables, which commanded high prices. True, our small military post was the only market, and as all supplies required to supplement the gardeners' stores were by reason of freight equally high-priced, I doubt if the men even succeeded in making a comfortable living.

With all its drawbacks life was very enjoyable. Though out of the question to go far, yet we explored the country within a radius of several miles. Neither game nor fish were found, but it was a pleasure to meet the strange characters with which that region abounded.

We indulged in one visit to our regimental friends at Camp Willow Grove. Everything was delightful when once there, but we had as usual a disagreeable time going. Two days were consumed on the way. The first night was spent at a stage station where all the strange and uncouth experiences of our Nevada journey were repeated. There was, however, a woman in this rough home who shared her bed with me ; but as it was originally intended only for one person, and we each had an infant to care for, it soon became a question of whether or not I, who occupied the side next the wall, should be shoved through it.

The thin boards of which the house was built were distinguished, as is all frontier lumber, by their ability to warp, and therefore proved a protection only from the rain, and not from the wind which blew through the knot-holes and cracks. The inclemency of the weather made matters worse. It was a fearful night! I mentally resolved never to spend another in that rickety house. We changed our route returning, and passed through Prescott.

About that time we began to rejoice in the prospect of additional stores being furnished by the commissary department. After striving for nearly two years to vary the monotony of our rations, we felt as if the promised treat, in the shape of chocolate, macaroni, prunes, raisins, and currants, would be almost too much of a luxury, and care must be exercised if indigestion was not desired.

How much we enjoyed the slight variety! The zest with which cook and I rang the changes on those different comestibles would seem really childish at the present day, when almost all varieties of canned goods and luxuries in the shape of grocers' supplies can be found at every military post, however small and remote.

The amount of pleasure which can be derived from the most insignificant sources seems incredible; but I attribute much of the happiness I found in army life to my delight in trivial matters. Then we all were so united in mutual interests. The officers, instead of being immersed in business cares, were ever ready to be amazed or amused, as the case might be, with the results of our industry, and absolute delight was manifested over the most trifling plan for social enjoyment, which doubled the pleasure.

I have for many years entertained the greatest

regard for physicians, because during our army life they displayed so warm an interest in my children. One of the merits of frontier residence is that little ones thrive so much better there than in a city, and rarely suffer from the many ailments to which town-bred children are subject. The interest they inspire in every one, especially the post surgeon, whose constant presence in cases of emergency gives one a feeling of comfort and security nothing else can afford, is very gratifying. The result, even in cases of severe illness, is usually complete recovery. Both parents and patients unavoidably benefit by the surroundings.

Our doctor at Camp Date Creek was a character so uncommon that my recollections of him can never be effaced. He was an Irishman, a grandnephew of John Philpot Curran, the distinguished Irish wit, and himself so full of humor that his very presence was an antidote to sickness and sorrow.

The doctor received a government contract after having been in America but a few months.

He never wearied of recounting the impressions American slang had made upon him. Immediately on entering our house he would seize baby and hold her for hours, all the time pouring forth reminiscences of Ireland, and expressing surprise at the difference between the two countries.

Our slang was described as very effective, especially the Californian, which had, or so the doctor assured me, a distinct vocabulary of its own, that, like adjectives, was capable of being positive, comparative, and superlative. As an example he instanced the following:

"You bet, you bet you, you bet your life." "Why," said he, "here is a perfect declension! You bet your boots, you bet your bottom dollar, you bet stamps."

The genial Irish doctor was immensely pleased with our vernacular, if with nothing else.

It would afford me much pleasure to prolong the narration of incidents connected with those friends who aided so greatly in making our life enjoyable, but I must hurry on with the account of our journey to New Mexico.

CHAPTER IX.

OUR little daughter was just eleven months old when the regiment was ordered to move. We started on our long journey in mid-winter. The troops from Prescott were to cross directly into New Mexico; and we had hoped to accompany them, but were instead sent to join others from the southern posts. That made our journey much longer, as after going in a southerly, then easterly direction, our line lay north to Fort Stanton, New Mexico.

Eve could hardly have felt more reluctant to leave the Garden of Eden than I did when we bade farewell to the camp, which though indeed desolate, never had seemed so to me, but, rather, the most delightful imaginable spot. I cried bitterly for days. My packing was accomplished with a heavy heart, I was so miserable at the thought of leaving that which had been my first real home.

We were to have no company for some days but that of the troop and our dear old captain, who was really like one of ourselves. His true and loving nature had greatly endeared him to us, and he formed a firm link in the family chain.

Unaccustomed to any comfort on former journeys, I was not inclined to exact much on that, so soon learned instinctively to fall into the regular routine and discipline, and expected no consideration on account of my sex. I had never before traveled with troops; and though I did not like to rise long before the first peep of day, and after a hurried and scanty breakfast climb into an ambulance and drive for hours, I soon learned to do so without a murmur. My reward came in the praise our captain bestowed, when he declared that during the entire march of six long, weary weeks, I had never caused one moment's delay or trouble.

I have often since questioned whether some

plan might not have been devised to prevent the officers' wives from being subjected to the stringent rules that must be enforced among soldiers. I suppose that just as a woman whose husband is in business regulates her household according to the needs or conveniences of its head, so, with the same spirit, the wife of an army officer endures the hardships her husband's position imposes.

Our beloved commanding officer had been in the army so many years that the possibility of deviating in any degree from the routine which had become second nature doubtless never occurred to him. Probably no question of expediency — simply that of duty — ever suggested itself.

Though a sufferer all my life from army discipline, which has continually controlled my movements, yet, when chafing most against its restraints, I have admired the grand soldierly spirit which made nearly every officer uncomplainingly forego all personal comfort for the sake of duty. No one outside the army can realize what the true soldier relinquishes when he forsakes home and family for the noble cause.

Every one has read or heard of the mad courage displayed in times of war, and my knowledge of the soldier is in times of peace; yet I have then seen exhibited what to me is by far the truer heroism. It is easy to be brave when war trumps sound and the spirit is roused to great hopes of personal achievements, when love for a cause deepens the ardor which sustains men even in death; but tame submission to petty and altogether unnecessary hardships, because in the line of duty and part of a soldier's inevitable fate, is, in my opinion, far more praiseworthy.

Our captain was a hero in the truest sense of the word. Like many others, he had served for years during our civil war as a private before being promoted to the rank of an officer. But after promotion the possession and exercise of rare soldierly qualities soon enabled him to reach a position of influence. He was intrusted with the command of a company, which after a desperate resistance was captured. Having been severely wounded, he was released on parole, and remained in a little town of Southern New Mexico, where he was well taken care of, and during that season of forced inactivity recovered his health.

Almost anyone would have considered him fairly entitled to pay; but such was his idea of rectitude that he refused to accept a dollar, not considering that it had been fairly earned; and to this day the five months' pay due him while a prisoner remains in the coffers of our government. The subsequent life of this honorable man has been one of duty and devotion to country. His health is ruined by the almost incredible hardships a cavalry soldier's duties entail.

We journeyed south through Arizona to Tucson, then turned east. Our outfit consisted of a wall tent, which on encamping at night was placed on as smooth ground as could be found, and a mess chest filled with supplies. By placing a support under the raised cover of the lat-

ter, and filling the open space with a board that
fitted nicely, it could be utilized as a table.
The interior contained plates and dishes in
addition to supplies, and the moment we reached
camp our cook, a soldier, would begin preparations for a meal, which though ever so plain
was always done full justice to by appetites the
long ride had sharpened.

In accordance with my usual habit, I made all
necessary preparations in advance for supplying
our wants; and it soon became more a question
of quantity than of quality, for the generous
hearts of Mr. Boyd and the captain always forgot that our supplies were limited. An instance of their thoughtlessness in such matters
was on one occasion evinced by the arrival,
unexpectedly to me, of four guests whom they
had invited to remain with us for a few days.
To supply food for a week — as it happened
in that case — to those extra people, blessed
with unusually good appetites, taxed my inge-
nuity.

We had by that time reached the celebrated

Indian villages of the Pimas and Maricopas. Those two tribes had been at peace with the pale faces for a century. They cultivated land, and were industrious and prosperous. Their villages stretched along the highway for many miles, so we spent six days among them. They watched our progress in the well-known, somewhat indifferent Indian fashion, though evincing real interest when we encamped at night, and swarming about us with various wares for sale, such as pottery and baskets, both unique in pattern and very serviceable. The latter were made so fine in texture and quality as to hold water. The various designs in which those useful articles were woven displayed much taste.

We felt that a land flowing with milk and honey had indeed been reached. Not only could eggs and chickens be bought, but so cheaply we could indulge in them to our hearts' content.

The Pima and Maricopa Indians, like all others, were unprepossessing in appearance;

but aware that after leaving them we would be once more among the murderous Apaches, I, for one at least, enjoyed their society because of the protection it afforded.

Every night when we pitched our tents the women would crowd about and indulge in ecstasies over the little white baby whose ablutions were a source of constant and serious wonderment. This can be well understood when one remembers that Indians rarely, if ever, use water other than for drinking purposes. I never permitted any of them to touch baby, being afraid to do so.

Our little Chinaman, with his long pigtail, also caused much amazement and no doubt speculation as to what he really was. As no attempt was made to disguise this, he evidently became at once disgusted with notoriety. It was, I believe, the cause of his one day appearing minus that appendage so revered by all Chinese — his cue. When I inquired what had become of it, and told him he could never return to China, he replied:

"Me no care. Me want to be 'Melican man."

Our baby was singularly fair and white; and in all our travels, both among Indians and Mexicans, all went into raptures over the children, who with their sunny heads were such utter contrasts to the swarthy races among which we moved.

A few days of travel after leaving the Indian villages brought us to Tucson, then an insignificant town of flat mud houses, so unprepossessing that we were glad to drive through without stopping, and encamp beside a beautiful stream two miles beyond. The town was then being decimated by small-pox, which raged among the Mexicans. We were obliged to flee from contact with it, especially as our soldiers were always ready to explore any new place, regardless of consequences.

We spent one day in sight seeing, though the only point of special interest was a noted church nine miles from Tucson. I cannot express the astonishment excited by the sight of that house

of worship built in those vast wilds, hundreds of
miles from all civilization.   The edifice, of noble
proportions, was of red brick and whitish stucco.
Both belfry and tower were complete.   The interior decorations were profuse, and covered the
walls.   The floor, once hard and smooth, had
been worn into hollows by the footsteps of
countless devotees, whose race even was unknown, though surmised to be that of the
ancient Aztecs, or followers of Montezuma.

I doubt if even in Europe, with its mystic
shrines dating back countless ages, I could have
experienced a more profound sense of awe than
when standing in that absolutely desert spot,
and realizing that skilled hands had once erected
there such a monument.

In that old church were marriage records dating back hundreds of years; but the structure
was to me the all absorbing wonder.

The Mexicans living near worshiped most
devoutly at its shrines; and they were not the
only frequenters of that house of prayer, for
the Spanish priests had a large following of

Indians who had intermarried with the Spaniards and settled there.

I could hardly tear myself from the spot, and returned again and again to ascend the belfry stairs and wonder and speculate upon the strange mystery called "San Xavier del Bac."

CHAPTER X.

AT that point we parted with our four guests, who had contributed, by their fund of wit and humor, to render the journey pleasant, and had added much to our merriment at meal times. It required, however, a stronger sense of humor than I possessed to be merry at breakfast, eaten in semi-darkness, after having been awakened with military precision.

It was certainly not cheerful to watch the tent and its furnishings disappear in the wagon while we sat trying to imagine ourselves breakfasting, with the sharp morning air of February chilling, or the March winds blowing about us. When the dreary meal was over we scrambled into our ambulance, and by the time a few miles had been passed I would be fairly awake and longing for lunch time.

The strangest part of those travels is that children thrive so well, and really enjoy every moment of the journey, however monotonous. My baby could not walk, and I was glad of it; for a more thorny, desolate country than that it has never been my lot to traverse. The innumerable beds of cacti were the spots most delighted in by children, and I rejoiced that baby had no chance of being lost among those dangerous plants.

After leaving Tucson, we passed many lonely graves dispersed over the weird desolation of that uninhabited space, and soon learned to discern where savage Apaches had moved. With our escort of fifty well-mounted men we had nothing to fear; but those mounds of stones, appealing in mute silence to the passer by, touched me deeply.

On arriving at the different stage stations we generally rested a while, and usually found there some poor woman who was working day and night to assist her husband, and with whom I always made it a custom to converse. The comparison of the lives of those women with mine caused me to feel additional sympathy for them, and gratitude on my own account.

Notwithstanding our large escort, it was necessary to proceed with great caution, for one never could tell what might happen when passing through the mountainous regions of Southern Arizona. Camp Bowie, at which we remained three days, was nestled amid high mountains, and Indians often appeared on the bluffs above, from which they fired recklessly and sometimes effectively. A large guard was always detailed to watch the outposts ; and yet so subtle, as is well known, are Indians, that although close at hand they were seldom caught.

One evening while we were at Camp Bowie an Indian crept into the stables, and while the sentry was pacing to and fro at the farther end, mounted a fine horse standing near the entrance, and with a yell of victory horse and rider disappeared. He well knew that once mounted, pursuit could be defied.

That strange little fort in the very heart of
the mountain fastness sheltered a number of
women and children. As usual, we received a
hearty welcome, and were feasted and *fêted* in
true army fashion. The post surgeon vacated
his room in our honor; for which we were very
grateful, especially when one of those terrible
mountain blizzards came on, in which clouds of
dust so thick are formed that objects cannot be
distinguished at a distance of ten feet. The
room we occupied was built of logs, and dust
blew through the crevices until it seemed as if
we were a part of the universal grit. The tents
were simply uninhabitable, though before our
destination was reached we were compelled to
occupy them through what seemed fully as
severe a storm.

Officers have the habit of beautifying their
quarters all circumstances permit; and our
friend the doctor, who had incommoded himself
for us, was no exception to the general rule.
The rough mud ceiling of his room had been
covered with unbleached cotton; and shelves,

mostly laden with books, were suspended from
rafters by means of the same material torn into
strips. One hanging over the open fireplace
was crowded with bottles of all sizes and descriptions, which contained every form of vermin and reptile life to be found in that region.
In the eyes of one unaccustomed to such sights
it would, indeed, have been an alarming display.

The collection embraced centipeds, scorpions,
tarantulas in their hideous blackness, and snakes
of all kinds — at least those small enough to
be bottled. They were not elegant mantel
ornaments, but having been long accustomed
to such sights I did not mind them. It was,
however, altogether another matter to be
brought in actual contact with the monstrosities, as happened on the second night of the
storm.

We were thoroughly worn out combating the
omnipresent dust, and had retired early, when
a tremendous crash suddenly awakened us from
sound sleep. At first we thought the end of
the world had come; but soon discovered that

the shelf containing bottled tenants had fallen.
It was some time before a light could be procured; for matches and lamps, as well as clocks
and watches, were all buried under the *débris.*

No description can do justice to the scene.
Everything upon the shelf, ornamental as well
as useful, formed a conglomerate mass, over
which the liberated monstrosities were scattered
in every direction.

The doctor apologized for the accident, but
we were none the worse, and it added one more
to the list of funny experiences that were often
afterward laughed over.

From Camp Bowie our road lay through grand
and gorgeous mountain scenery to Fort Cummings, in south-western New Mexico. A mountain pass on that route has been the scene of
more Indian atrocities than any other spot in
the entire Apache region. Magnificent Cook's
Peak has looked down upon more outrages
than time can ever efface. The stage road
wound through this pass for years, and the
number of times the Indians have brutally mur-

dered passengers is countless. Even now that a railroad has superseded the stage, it is a place of terror to most travelers, and the history of its bloody battles and massacres would fill volumes.

We remained at Fort Cummings one day, and found it indeed a wretched place, devoid of all attractions save the kind friends who made us so welcome.

Another day's march brought us to Fort Selden, on the Rio Grande, from whence we caught our first glimpse of that strange river. Rising in Southern Colorado, a beautifully clear stream, it flows on for hundreds and hundreds of miles, changing color as frequently as does the famous chameleon. Now it is bright and sparkling, again dull and sluggish, and anon disappears completely, to reappear with added volume and intensity. How many have been deceived by that treacherous river! Trusting to its apparently listless course, travelers have been suddenly swept away in a mad, headlong current, which absorbed their lives as the vampire is said to do those of his prey. Ah! if the casualties that have occurred on the Rio Grande could be written, each of its victims adding but one line to the record, what a strange and fearful story would be told.

There is a tradition to the effect that any one tasting its waters will be compelled, by some strange, subtle charm or influence, to return, even though after the lapse of years. Certain it is that people always long to again experience its strange and weird fascination, which seems really to follow them, and from which there is no respite until the mighty stream is actually revisited.

The Rio Grande, which I first saw twenty years ago, has often charmed me since. Though not often again in the same region, I have elsewhere followed its banks for miles, and the borders of no other river it has ever been my fortune to gaze upon, present so many varieties of life. Desolation and beautiful verdure are mingled; while its fruitful produce tends to make the country, which without its beneficent influence would indeed be a desert, a very paradise.

But I would not forestall my narrative by saying too much of this river, to which I so often returned, and which finally became like a familiar friend, a part of my very life itself.

We left the Rio Grande at Don Aña, and struck off into beautiful, piney Lincoln County, New Mexico, where we had a happy home for another year. Before reaching there we encamped for one night at White Sands, memorable on account of the peculiarity of its soil. A perfectly wonderful mass of pure white sand, which lay in hillocks, extended far as the eye could reach. We climbed onward, our feet sinking in slightly, just enough to remind us of "footsteps on the sands of time." Those sand hillocks had existed from time immemorial, and will remain for ages to come, I suppose, unless some commercial mind shall divine their value and utilize the white commodity, by converting it into a merchantable article. I am glad to have seen them in their spotless purity and beauty.

The remainder of our journey to dear old Fort Stanton was through exquisite forests of mountain pines, and beside clear streams that yielded delicious trout.

CHAPTER XI.

AT Fort Stanton nature was a constant source of joy and pleasure. The near-by streams were fairly alive with delicious fish, so abundant that a line could hardly be thrown before one would bite. Besides fish, we had game of almost every variety, and fairly lived on the " fat of the land." New Mexico had been called " The Troopers' Paradise," and we found the name to be well merited.

Perhaps the very wildness of the country and abundance of game provoked a lawless element; for Lincoln County, if a good one for natural supplies, has always been regarded as a rallying point for desperadoes, and its history is famous in the annals of crime.

At first my wonder and sympathies were excited; but in time the peaceful security one always experiences when surrounded by well-armed troops deadened susceptibilities to what transpired outside. Army officers' wives hear of bloodshed with much the same feeling as is experienced by women living in cities when they learn of frightful accidents which involve the lives of others, but of none who are near and dear to them.

We passed one happy, peaceful year at Fort Stanton. The houses, built of stone, which was very plentiful in that mountainous region, were very comfortable. Each had two rooms, with a detached kitchen and dining-room about fifteen feet in the rear.

The climate was perfect, the air so exquisitely pure as to lend a freshness and charm to each day's existence. To breathe was like drinking new wine. I cannot pity the isolation of settlers in those regions, for the beauty of natural scenery displayed on all sides is ample compensation, and to live is to enjoy. My recollections of that year are delightful.

Several companies had preceded us, so I had

companions of my own sex. Our amusements consisted in part of driving, and fishing in streams where success, however inferior the angler's skill, was certain. Our wildest gayety was a card-party, and we always attended military balls. There were not enough officers' wives to have dances of our own; but we always opened those of the soldiers', and thoroughly appreciated their enjoyment.

Some of those affairs would have presented a strange picture to people in the East; but the very absurdity and variety of the costumes and conduct of frontiersmen and their wives, who were always invited, only added zest to our enjoyment, and the recollections amused us for days.

One evening so fierce a storm raged that we hardly dared cross the parade ground; yet our desire to go was sufficient to induce the attempt. We were fairly blown into the room, and to our surprise found it filled with the usual throng. How in the world they had all reached the place through such a severe storm puzzled us greatly, but there they were.

It was a curious sight, and a still more curious sound, that all those people produced. The strains of music, the stamping of many feet, and the wild howling of the wind, all combined to greatly stimulate our nerves. The excitement was still further increased when suddenly a loud crash was heard; every one rushed out in alarm to discover that a huge flagstaff, which it had taken months to make and erect, had fallen and been splintered into a thousand fragments. The staff had not been properly secured by stanchions.

The occurrence was regretted, not only because the making and erecting had consumed much time, but also because it had been difficult to find a suitable tree tall enough for the purpose. Thus our towering flagstaff, which had taken many years to grow and several months to fashion, had been laid low in a less number of seconds.

Soon after I experienced another fright, quite

different in its nature from the one just related. I now firmly believe an army garrison to be the most secure place on earth, and in later years almost forgot the use of keys; but in those earlier days I was always on the alert.

One night when Mr. Boyd was away I placed a student lamp at the foot of our bed, and after looking under it in the usual approved woman fashion, lay down to rest. My nervous fears had only just passed away, permitting me to fall into a light slumber, when I found myself suddenly sitting up gazing at the form of a man entering the door. My heart seemed to stop beating, yet fortunately I had the courage to exclaim:

"What are you doing here? Leave the room!"

The man promptly obeyed. I sprang up, locked the door, and called the servants. When I found that my nurse, who slept in the next room, had disappeared, and that cook, on account of the distance between the house and kitchen, could not hear me, I felt as if a plan was on foot to murder me, and endured a half-hour of absolute agony, such as I hope it will never again be my lot to experience.

At last the nurse appeared, and I went once more to rest; but so vivid were my impressions of the man that I picked him out next day from among a hundred; and then begged, on learning that he had been wandering around intoxicated, and merely entered the first door which responded to his touch, that no punishment be inflicted.

Beautiful Fort Stanton was not only perfect in natural scenery and surroundings, but had been improved by excellent methods. Various officers had from time to time planted trees around the parade ground; and to facilitate their growth an *acequia*, as it was called in Spanish, or ditch, had been dug, and the water, constantly running through it, kept the roots of the trees always moist, so they grew rapidly and formed a delightful shade in front of our quarters.

We became so fond of our home in that

charming spot that everything else contented us. The mail came, as before, but once a week, and its arrival made that day a red-letter one in our quiet lives. It was always devoted to eager anticipations and close watching of the long line of road over which the mail rider came. If over due, nothing else could be thought or talked of until he arrived, and we received our news from beyond the border. Even baby learned to look for letters, and to expect some token of love from absent friends. She would forsake her favorite playground near the muddy *acequia* to join the anxious group of watchers.

Every one has heard the story of the baby who was taken by her mother to some perform- ance in San Francisco in the early days, when women were scarce and babies so rare as almost to be wonders; and how, when the little one cried and refused to be pacified, an old miner arose and requested that the play should cease so they might hear the baby cry. His request was applauded on all sides, and a hat passed round for the baby, who had reminded those rough men of a home life almost forgotten in their pioneer surroundings.

My baby was not only of the greatest importance to me, but if I noticed any sign of the devotion she was expected to receive from other sources flagging, my displeasure was quickly expressed. I have since been told that the officers, after reporting for duty to their commander, would say :

"Now we must go see baby, and report her condition."

Consequently she received as much notice as if it had been her divine right. The little one could talk plainly by the time she was fifteen months old, and amused us all greatly.

In looking back upon those happy days I often wonder how I could voluntarily have left so dear a home. But after residing there a year I decided to visit friends in New York, so bade farewell to beautiful Fort Stanton, not knowing I never should again see it.

CHAPTER XII.

WE left Fort Stanton in March, prepared for a seemingly almost interminable journey before reaching the railroad at Denver, five hundred miles distant. Expecting to find houses in which to pass the nights, we took no tent, and besides my trunk very little baggage. It was entirely too early in the season for traveling to be really comfortable, as in that exquisite mountain air mornings and evenings are very cold.

The country between Forts Stanton and Union was simply superb in its wild grandeur and beauty. Only the pen of an artist could have done justice to its many charms. We stopped every night with Mexican families, who in their simple kindness were most truly hospitable. They made us welcome, and yet exacted no reward for the time and attention bestowed. I always required those hours for rest and looking after baby, who with the happy unconcern of childhood had a way of wandering in paths unsuited to such tender feet.

In all those rough travels I never met with anything else which gave me so much trouble as the cactus plant. Wherever we went, and whatever else we missed, that was always present in some shape or form. In regions where nothing else could be prevailed upon to grow, that useful but disagreeable plant always throve; and the more dreary, parched, and barren the soil, the more surely did the cactus flourish and expand its bayonet-armed leaves.

If very young children were allowed to wander in the least, one could safely depend upon finding them in the vicinity of the dangerous cacti. During that journey our little one tripped and fell directly upon a large plant, which, it seemed to me, had more than the usual complement of thorns, for her little knees were fairly filled with them, and days passed before all were picked out.

Cacti are the main feature of Western plant life. Sometimes with fluted columns, as in Arizona, they rear their heads aloft in stately grandeur. Again they are found in some one of the numerous less inspiring shapes and forms the plant assumes in different parts of the West. There must be at least fifty varieties. All are supplied with that chief characteristic — sharp-pointed prickers — which remind the unwary of their presence and power.

It takes a great deal of frontier experience to deal correctly with cacti. They have many and valuable properties which the early settlers long since discovered. The most common variety is the low, flat-land species which requires no seeking. In the far West it flaunts itself by all roadsides and everywhere dots the prairies. It is very nutritive, and utilized by natives as food for cattle; they first burn away the prickles with which it has been so bountifully supplied by nature. Even in that land of seeming bar-

renness for man and beast, much can be found
to support life. The cactus supplies an intoxicating liquor called *mescal;* and one variety
bears a fruit which tastes somewhat like the
strawberry, and is much sought after by Mexicans.

The only time when cacti are really pretty
is in early spring, when they bloom. Then the
bright-hued flowers dot the country with color,
and relieve the eye from the monotonous gray
hue which pervades all nature in a region where
rains are so periodical as to prevent the vernal
freshness of the East.

There is a rare and nameless charm in the
contemplation of those extended prairies, with
their soft gray tints, dreary to Eastern people,
but so dearly loved by those who become im-
bued with the deep sentiment their vast expanse
inspires.

I shall never become reconciled to localities
where the eye cannot look for miles and miles
beyond the spot where one stands, and where
the density of the atmosphere circumscribes the

view, limiting it to a comparatively short distance. I have traveled in New Mexico and Arizona for days, when on starting early in the morning the objective point of my journey, and an endless stretch of road, perhaps for a hundred miles, could be seen.

To mount a horse, such as can be found only in the West, perfect for the purpose, and gallop over prairies, completely losing one's self in vast and illimitable space, as silent as lonely, is to leave every petty care, and feel the contented frame of mind which can only be produced by such surroundings. In those grand wastes one is truly alone with God. Oh, I love the West, and dislike to think that the day will surely come when it will teem with human life and all its warring elements !

On that journey East from my dear Western home everything seemed new. After traveling for days, Fort Union was reached, where we remained a while, and then went North, passing through beautiful Colorado, stopping at Trinidad, Pueblo, and finally, after seventeen days of ambulance travel, reaching Denver. It was more like a panoramic journey than a real one; for we kept continually advancing toward a higher and higher degree of civilization, till its apex — New York — was reached.

All those strange, crude, and uncivilized Western villages have since become thriving railroad towns. Denver, with its perfect environment of exquisite mountain scenery, will always remain in my mind a picture of beauty.

Mr. Boyd was to leave me at Denver, and return to Fort Stanton; but we first spent a delightful week there. My brother met and introduced us to some pleasant people. There was a fine company at the principal theatre, which we attended nightly, and I shed tears over dear old Rip Van Winkle, who, though not personated by Jefferson, was sufficiently well portrayed to merit and receive great applause. The absolute freshness of feeling one experiences after years of absence from such scenes is sufficiently delightful to make the jaded theater-goer envious.

I was exceedingly proud of my introduction to that estimable couple, Mr. and Mrs. McKee Rankin, the " stars " in that theatrical combination ; and we were honored by an invitation to dine with them, which was accepted. We had the pleasantest imaginable time.

My brother had been living in Cheyenne for some time, and, in his great desire to again witness a fine theatrical performance, had, with a friend, assumed the entire responsibility of the troupe's success. A week had been spent in enlisting every one's interest; and although he guaranteed expenses in any event, yet when the important night arrived there was a full house, and one of the most picturesque audiences ever collected. Every miner, ranchman, gambler, and the whole military garrison at Cheyenne, were not only there, but applauded everything as a Western audience alone can — in a manner that made the very building tremble.

Such an audience is a sight which once seen is not easily forgotten. Similar heterogeneous elements never enter into the lives of the people at the East, and it is almost impossible to describe such a gathering. Imagine a peculiarly picturesque and large audience, composed of every imaginable species of the human race, each so intent upon the performance that actual surroundings are entirely ignored.

In those early days of which I am writing, the population of Denver was much more composite than it is at the present time; and the experienced eye could readily distinguish men and women of every nationality, and from every station in life, from the cowboy to the millionaire. Beautiful Denver! my heart turns longingly to its perfect climate; and the desire to once again inhale that sweet, pure air, and catch a glimpse of its glorious mountain scenery, cannot be overcome.

We left that lovely town after a week's delightful stay, and for two days and nights rolled over the prairies in cars, watching the endless stretch of level and monotonous plains, relieved here and there by herds of buffaloes, which sometimes approached so near as to be shot at from the train. It reminded me of the excitement created when whales are encountered on a sea voyage, because the passengers, after once having seen them, were constantly on the lookout for more, and the state of expectancy rendered their journey less tedious. These herds of buffaloes have long since disappeared from the Kansas plains, and their very memory will soon become a recollection of the past.

As we rolled into dingy St. Louis, where brother left me, my heart sank at the prospect of again breathing air too heavy and dense to be anything but suffocating. The next morning found me in Chicago, where I was to be met by another brother. Our little daughter was so accustomed to being on friendly terms with every one, that she used to go from one end of the car to the other, chatting and enjoying every moment of her trip. To ride in cars, after lurching about in all sorts of uncomfortable conveyances over rough mountains and plains, was like gently gliding; and but for the heavy atmosphere and coal dust, it seemed as if I should never tire.

A very enjoyable day was passed in Chicago. My brother pointed out, with evident pride, the splendid public buildings, which but a few months later were devastated by the fire fiend, only to rise, phœnix-like, from their ruins in greater beauty and splendor.

I have the most profound admiration both for Chicago and the spirit of enterprise shown by its inhabitants; and when I saw it again after the calamity, I bowed in reverence to a community that could evolve so much architectural beauty and elegance, to say nothing of comfort, from so disastrous a misfortune as that terrible fire.

Twenty hours after leaving Chicago found me in New York. I had looked forward with intense longing to that moment, supposing ineffable happiness would be my portion when again there; but standing in front of the Fifth Avenue hotel, a landmark more familiar to me than any other in the city, my disappointment and heart sickness were severe.

I had seen the hotel rise from nothing; had

always lived in the immediate vicinity, daily passed it going to and from school; and when homesick during my army life the mere thought of that hotel would awaken the happiest feelings; but when the desire to again see it had been attained my heart sank with a bitter feeling of loneliness.

No longing has ever equaled in intensity the one which then took possession of me — to be back again in my dear Western home, surrounded by all the lonely grandeur of its lovely scenery. Though I remained East an entire year, it was only because obliged to, and during all those months I never ceased to sigh for the day of my return.

I had many joyful reunions with kind relatives and dear friends, much to make life bright and cheerful; but I raved about the delights of the West until friends thought me nearly crazy on the subject. Besides missing my own home, as do all married women, in spite of the unbounded hospitality of friends, I missed the quiet and freedom from that mad rush which seems an inevitable part of life in a great city. I was also in the hands of physicians, which was depressing. The hardships of frontier life, at times when I was entirely unfitted for travel, had told their tale, and compelled my return East in order that my shattered health might be regained.

Three months were spent in New York, and then, with the approach of warm weather, I wended my way to the mountains. Although they seemed insipid after the rocky grandeur of the West, I preferred them, such as they were, to the city with its endless streets and turmoil, where tall chimney tops prevented my obtaining a glimpse of the blue sky I had seen so freely and loved so well.

CHAPTER XIII.

I DOUBT if any but those who have lived among the prairies or mountains of the far West can realize how keenly is felt the loss of that endless environment which becomes a part of life itself, and which is missed when deprived of, especially at first, almost like one's daily bread.

From the city I went to my husband's home in New York State, on a spur of the Catskill Mountains, where I seemed to breathe more freely, and was enchanted during those long summer months by the exquisite green of grass, trees, and landscape — in a word, by every thing that refreshed the eye after such a long period of gray hues, and which certainly my beloved West lacked.

I was enthusiastic over the fresh verdure of

our beautiful mountain home, just as I had
been over the gray loveliness of the West. It
was, no doubt, the marked contrast which gladdened my eyes. Not a moment was spent
in-doors if it could be avoided; and when compelled to do so, I placed myself where a perpetual feast to the eyes was in full view.

One could dwell perpetually amid recollections of the past; so I will hasten over that
quiet, restful summer to the succeeding fall,
when my husband arrived on his first leave of
absence. Needless to say the young soldier
was greeted by his family with the welcome
befitting one, who, having spent three years in
distant service, returned to his home with un-
alloyed pleasure, and reviewed with renewed
delight the early surroundings and memories of
his youth.

During the month following Mr. Boyd's arrival our first boy was born, and no prince could
ever have been received with more sincere delight. Parents and grandparents were unanimous in considering him wonderful, and indeed

he was a splendid baby! My husband celebrated his advent as we would have done on the frontier, with much rejoicing; but the Puritan grandparents seriously objected to conviviality of any kind, and seized the occasion to obtain their son's promise to abstain in future from intoxicating liquors of every description. To gratify his dear father Mr. Boyd agreed, although there was no necessity for such a pledge, as he had always been most temperate. Our son was ten years of age before Captain Boyd again tasted liquor, and then it was by the doctor's express order.

When our baby boy was three months old his father began to think the country a cold place for us, and to debate the desirability of a return to New York, especially as he felt we were entitled, after our long sojourn on the frontier, to some of the pleasures of Eastern life. One entire morning was spent in discussing the matter. The conclusion arrived at was, that even if we remained with relatives the amount of my husband's pay would in no wise suffice for the ordinary expenses of life in New York. In order to have any leisure I should require a nurse for our two little children, and the half-pay received was only sixty-five dollars a month.

In relating these experiences of army life, I wish it distinctly understood that I am not exaggerating—simply stating facts. A cavalry officer was deprived of almost every opportunity of visiting home and relatives in the East, and when permitted to do so on leave was compelled to plunge in debt, which involved him for years afterward in difficulties: so, great as was the pleasure, and most innocent and natural, we considered it too dearly bought ever to be repeated, and therefore did not again come East until compelled to do so on account of our children's education.

My husband had journeyed from Fort Stanton to New York at frightful expense, traveling by stage to Denver, which, as my previous experience has shown, was the most costly mode of transit. An officer has not only to make all trips when on leave at his own expense, but in those days the pay was reduced to half its full amount; and as a lieutenant was then allowed only one hundred and thirty dollars, Mr. Boyd received but sixty-five dollars a month. Such reduction seems to me most unjust, for surely no one can be expected to spend a lifetime away from all early associations, or pay so dearly for the natural desire to occasionally see parents and friends.

We were indeed happy with the pleasure of again visiting our relatives; but when the long, long return journey from New York to New Mexico had to be undertaken, and we found that with the utmost economy it would cost seven hundred dollars, which, with the limited supply of household necessaries absolutely required, and the expenses of Mr. Boyd's journey East added, aggregated upwards of thirteen hundred dollars, it was anything but a pleasant outlook for the future. We were in debt to that amount, and must provide for its payment.

Can any one wonder either at our dismay, or the resolve never again to think of leave of ab-

sence? For economy we had actually buried
ourselves in the mountains during the entire
winter; and although that was no great hardship, yet it would have been very pleasant to
have enjoyed New York during the season, especially as I never expected to come East again.

We realized the stern fact that with an in-
come of only sixty-five dollars a month, four
people should be thankful to have the bare necessaries of life, without expecting luxuries; but
it did seem rather hard to return without seeing
more of the city than a fleeting glimpse obtained
in passing, and — because we were poor.

While in New York one of my cousins found
a servant willing to return West with us, which
seemed desirable, as a nurse would be needed
on that long journey, and the amount of her
traveling expenses would be saved in the wages
to be paid — those current in New York instead
of the double rate demanded on the frontier.

We congratulated ourselves on the servant's
appearance, which was so far from pleasing it
seemed safe to take her. Had it been otherwise

she would, we were sure, soon desert us for matrimony. The girl was almost a grenadier in looks and manners; and although not absolutely hideous, was so far from pleasing that we were confident of retaining her services, so made a contract for one year.

Our Western journey was uneventful in comparison with others that had preceded it. It seemed a slight undertaking to travel with our two little children, who were so good and healthy, and I had the assistance both of my husband and the nurse. Besides, the joy experienced at being fairly *en route* for our own home made me feel like a caged bird let loose.

After four days and nights of travel from the East into the West, we reached Cheyenne, Wyoming Territory, where the children, nurse, and I were to remain with my brother, while Mr. Boyd went to New Mexico by stage, and returned with an ambulance for our long journey.

My heart swells when I think of those per-

fect days! It was in the month of May, and
we either camped out every night, or slept in
some ranch. Each moment was fraught with
pleasure. Every whiff of mountain air was in-
haled with delight, for, like a Mohammedan, my
face was turned toward Mecca. I so rejoiced
that our nurse, who was undergoing the same
disagreeable sensations I had experienced at the
outset of my army life in the strange surroundings, was so overpowered she dared not express
her dissatisfaction.

On arriving at Trinidad, a halt was made,
for I had forgotten to check our trunks from
Denver to Kit Carson, so they did not follow.
We awaited them there for a while, but finally
decided to go on. When the trunks eventually
reached us, we discovered that they had been
left standing somewhere in the rain until their
contents were saturated with water and had
mildewed.

I felt badly enough over my own trunk; but
the nurse wept, "refusing to be comforted," for
all her finery was ruined. My own regrets

were silenced in listening to her lamentations, especially as I was entirely to blame.

We did not return to Fort Stanton, Mr. Boyd's company having been ordered to Fort Union ; so the journey, which I regarded in the light of a picnic, from the railroad to our home, required only twelve days. It was delightful in every respect, or would have been but for the sour face of our nurse, " who mourned, and mourned, and mourned."

When we reached Fort Union, and I asked if it would not be a pleasant home for us, she looked out on the wide and desolate plain that faced the fort, and with a weary sigh, said she "preferred New York."

Having known the pangs of homesickness, I sympathized with her deeply ; but she kept up so continuously her wail of despair over the discomforts of our life generally, and it became so tiresome, that when, five months afterward, she married a soldier, I was rather glad than otherwise, and returned with a sense of relief to the faithful men for service.

We had soon discovered the fallacy of our belief that her plainness would prevent the possibility of a lover. Women were so scarce, and
men so plenty, that no matter how old or ugly,
a woman was not neglected, and our unprepossessing nurse had scores of suitors for her hand.
She had not been in the fort three days before
the man who laid our carpets proposed to her.
It required but little time in which to become
aware of her own value, and on learning
that he was intemperate she quickly discarded
him.

The one whom she finally married was brave
in every sense of the word. Trusting to the
old adage, "Faint heart ne'er won fair ladie,"
that man engaged a carriage at Las Vegas for
the wedding-trip before ever having seen her.
He was a soldier belonging at Fort Union, who
had been away on distant service for months,
and, hearing that we had a girl from the East
with us, made the necessary preparations for
their marriage while *en route* to the post. His
pluck must have pleased her, for three days

after his return she accompanied him to Las Vegas, where they were united for life.

She had made my life harder in every way, and taught us the folly of taking a servant accustomed to Eastern civilization into the Western wilds. Not only had she scorned all our belongings and surroundings, but absolutely wearied me with incessant complaints over the absence of modern conveniences, which was absurd; for the climate was so exquisite, and the houses so compact, there was really no necessity for such fretfulness. We had clean, sweet, fresh quarters, which to me seemed perfect.

So greatly, however, had the girl deplored the situation, that I wondered she thought to better her condition by marrying a soldier, who can often give his wife no shelter whatever; in fact, unless permitted to marry by the consent of his officers, she is not allowed to live in the garrison.

That was a hard summer in spite of my joy at our return. Mr. Boyd had been ordered to join his troop in the field immediately after our arrival. I had a dear little house, and with new carpets and curtains, and the absolute freshness of all, would have been happy enough but for the load of debt that was constantly worrying me, and the discontent of our servant, which made her incapable to such a degree that I had to work so hard the flesh and strength gained by my pleasant Eastern visit greatly decreased. Before the summer was over I had lost twenty-five pounds.

Our dear captain had taken unto himself a bride, and in accordance with the usual army experience had been ordered away immediately on reaching the post, where he had hoped to enjoy his wife's society at least for a while. But the fortunes of war are ever the same, and our garrison was denuded of cavalry, which pursued Indians all summer. The officers always had so many comical stories to tell on their return, that even the bride failed to realize her husband's danger, and joined in the general laugh over those recitals.

One night the Indians actually invaded camp, and the officers were obliged to fight in their night clothes, having no time even to slip on shoes, but rushed immediately into the inclosure, that when camping was always formed by the wagons, and within which the animals were led. Having succeeded in driving off the Indians they laughed immoderately at each other, and considered the whole affair a great joke. The colonel was unusually tall, the quartermaster short and very stout, and each must have presented a comical appearance, fighting for dear life in such attire.

When absent on those expeditions the troop usually encamped on the banks of some stream. On one occasion the river by which they had camped rose — agreeably to the frequent custom of Western rivers — and carried away everything on its banks. When it fell their huge blacksmith's forge was found imbedded in the opposite shore, an eighth of a mile lower down.

The rainy season in those south-western countries is mostly confined to a few months, either in early spring or midsummer; and as no warning precedes its coming, sad accidents not infrequently occur. Sometimes in the course of a few hours a tiny little stream grows into an angry, surging torrent, so great is the downpour even in that short time. One dear woman, an officer's wife, who was camped with her husband on the banks of a river apparently in full security, lost her life from that cause.

A storm arose so suddenly, that, seeing their camp would soon be under water, she took shelter in an ambulance, to be driven across the stream to higher ground; but the treacherous current had grown so swift and strong that she and their child, together with the driver and mules, were swept away before the eyes of her husband, who stood agonized and helpless on the shore.

CHAPTER XIV.

WE were always delighted to welcome back the troops from their Indian reconnoitering, life was so dull without them. During their absence the garrison would consist perhaps of only one company of infantry, with its captain and lieutenant; and if at headquarters a quartermaster and an adjutant, with of course a doctor, who was our mainstay, and to whom we rushed if only a finger ached. That summer even the band was in the field, so we had no music to cheer us. All was, however, made up for on their return in November, when we inaugurated a series of hops that were delightful.

The quarters at Fort Union had an unusually wide hall which was superb for dancing, and three rooms on each side. We had only to notify the quartermaster that a hop was to be given, when our barren hallway would immediately be transferred into a beautiful ballroom, with canvas stretched tightly over the floor, flags decorating the sides, and ceiling so charmingly draped as to make us feel doubly patriotic.

Many ladies greatly dislike Fort Union. It has always been noted for severe dust-storms. Situated on a barren plain, the nearest mountains, and those not very high, three miles distant, it has the most exposed position of any military fort in New Mexico.

The soil is composed of the finest and, seemingly, lightest brown sand, which when the wind blows banks itself to a prodigious height against any convenient object. The most exposed place was between two sets of quarters, which were some distance apart. The wind would blow from a certain direction one day, and completely bank the side of one house ; the next it would shift, when the sand would be found lying against the other.

The hope of having any trees, or even a

grassy parade-ground, had been abandoned long before our residence there; for either the grass-seed would be scattered by the wind, or the grass actually uprooted and blown away after it had grown.

In 1886, when I again visited Fort Union, it seemed indeed a cheerless place on account of the lack of verdure. The cause is simply want of shelter; for with the ample water-works which have been built since we lived there, much could be done if it were in a less exposed position.

Those sand-banks were famous playgrounds for the children. One little girl, whose mother was constantly upbraiding her for lack of neatness, contrasting her with our little daughter who was almost painfully tidy, determining to be avenged, coaxed my child near a large sand-pile and threw her down on it, saying, as she again and again poured the dirt over her:

"There, now! I am glad to see you as dirty as I am!"

Every eye is said to form its own beauty.

Mine was disposed to see much in Fort Union, for I had a home there.

When my husband returned from his long scout we rode horseback daily. Our objective point was always the mountains, where trees and green grass were to be found in abundance. One day when in the Turkey mountains, about three miles from home, we saw two very ugly-visaged men approaching. Some instinct, or kind Providence, warned Mr. Boyd to keep a watchful eye on them, so he deliberately turned in the saddle, and placing one hand on a pistol to show that he was armed, watched them out of sight. One of the men, who turned back and looked at us, also rested a hand on his hip where the pistol is carried. Observing that we were intently watching their movements, they rode on, leaving us unmolested.

On our return we were greeted with the tale of a horrible murder that had been committed on the very outskirts of the post. A soldier messenger, who for ten years had carried the mail between Fort Union and the arsenal, a mile distant, had been shot within fifteen hundred yards of the garrison, and fallen lifeless by the roadside. His horse, instead of being captured by the murderers as they had hoped, galloped wildly toward the arsenal, and thus raised an alarm. The murderers were actually in sight when the poor man's body was found, still warm, but with life extinct.

A pursuing party was organized without loss of time, and on that open, level plain the wretches were almost immediately captured and placed in the guard-house. Mr. Boyd at once visited them, and found, as he expected, that they were the same men whom we had met in the mountains only a few hours previously. They would not, of course, reply to his query why they did not kill us for the sake of the fine horses we rode. He felt certain the murderers would be dealt with as summarily, and told them so, as had been the poor messenger whom they so foully murdered, and whose family was then suffering the most poignant sorrow.

Late that evening the civil authorities demanded the prisoners. Their only safety lay in the commanding officer refusing the request; but claiming that he had no authority for so doing, they were delivered to the sheriff, though begging and pleading to be permitted to remain in the guard-house. The men dreaded lynch law, but saw no mercy in the faces of their jailers.

After proceeding a short distance from the garrison, their escort increased in numbers until soon an immense crowd surrounded them. Not a sound was heard until the very verge of the military reservation had been reached, yet a more resolute and relentless body of men never marched together.

The very moment the last foot of military ground had been passed the sheriff was overpowered, evidently with no very great reluctance; and the crowd, producing coils of rope, quickly proceeded to hang the prisoners to telegraph-poles, where their bodies dangled for days, a warning to all horse thieves and murderers.

For a time my rides were spoiled; but soon I grew brave again, though we were always thereafter careful to be thoroughly well armed on leaving home.

I might multiply accounts of our experiences at various garrisons, but it would take too long. In a monotonous life days slip away almost unconsciously, and one is surprised to find how quickly time has flown. Looking back, it seems incredibly short, because there were no important events to mark its progress.

We were so happily situated that I hoped to remain at Fort Union, but as usual springtime saw us on the wing. It was undoubtedly a high compliment to my husband that he should always have been chosen as an administrative officer. It not only proved Mr. Boyd's ability, but was a testimony to his honesty, and thus a complete refutation of the charges made against him at West Point. It was also a special honor to be singled out from among so many men by the general in command at distant headquarters; but an inconvenience, particularly when we were at a very desirable post or station, to be ordered to a most uncomfortable one. Fort Union seemed far enough from the railroad, especially as our year East had made us anxious to be as near civilization as possible.

We were looking forward to a long stay at our pleasant post, when an unexpected order came for Mr. Boyd to proceed immediately to Fort Bayard, and build the officers' quarters needed there. He kept the news from me during the day of its arrival, because I was deeply engrossed in preparations for a hop to be given at our house that evening, and he did not wish to spoil my pleasure.

The entire day had been spent in decorating the hall and preparing supper. Unfortunately the first guest who arrived effectually dampened my spirits by sympathetically exclaiming :

" Isn't it too bad you have to leave here ? "

I was too unhappy to enjoy a single moment of the festivities which followed ; but the arrival of the entire garrison, who danced and otherwise greatly enjoyed themselves, left in my mind a picture of pleasant army gayety surpassed by none.

As usual I packed our household belongings with a heavy heart. That move was decidedly for the worse; and even if the journey, with its attendant fatigue and expense, had not been dreaded, I would have disliked going to a place so much farther from the railroad, and where so little could be expected in the way of comfort.

Fort Bayard, six hundred miles south-west of Fort Union, and a few miles distant from Arizona, was considered a most undesirable locality, both on account of its remoteness, and because no houses had then been built for the officers' use. It required eighteen days to reach our destination by ambulance, traveling about thirty-five miles each day.

After leaving Fort Union we went directly to Santa Fé, and saw that quaint old Mexican town, then across to Albuquerque, down by the borders of the Rio Grande to Fort Selden, and from there by ascending grades to Fort

Bayard, which was in the more mountainous region.

The journey was like all others in which ambulances were used as conveyances — tiresome and monotonous in the extreme, but in my case always either modified or intensified by the gladness or reluctance experienced in regard to our destination. In that case I was heartily sorry for the move. We had been only nine months at Fort Union ; my baby was at a troublesome age and needed constant care, and for the first time I was without a nurse of any sort. Besides, it was mid-winter, and unusual care must be exercised to keep the children warm when camping out, which we were compelled to do a part of the time. The season was, however, too cold to permit of that when it could be avoided, so we occupied Mexican houses almost every night.

The houses were very warm and comfortable, but oddly arranged according to American ideas. In place of windows there were merely openings for air, tightly closed or covered by solid wooden shutters at night. Several beds were ranged about the walls of each long, oddly shaped room, which except for a primitive wash-stand contained no other furniture. There was, however, always an open fireplace and a cheer-ful blaze of mesquite roots, which emitted much heat, and a curious odor that one never forgets.

The food was always enjoyed, for after long, open-air rides no one is ever very fastidious. Mexican cooking is not usually relished by those unaccustomed to it, because always highly flavored with garlic, much soaked in grease, and almost everything deluged with red pepper, without a lavish use of which no Mexican can prepare a single dish.

The most primitive mode of grinding corn — by hand between two stones — was then still in vogue; and the tortillas made from meal thus obtained, simply mixed with water and baked, were not only very sweet, but strange to say also light, probably because of the man-ipulation by skilled hands. They reminded me of the delicious beaten biscuits prepared in the

South, which are never fit to be eaten anywhere else.

The Rio Grande again became our constant companion, and we drove for days within sight of its banks. How I envied the Mexicans who were able to spend their lives on its sunny shores. Volumes could be written about those peculiar people, with their almost deathlike calm of manner, seldom, under any circumstances, varied; though sometimes the fact is betrayed that volcanic fires slumber beneath, to be fully roused and find vent only when their deepest emotions are stirred.

When living among them one feels the necessity of absorbing some of their traits, which are indeed needed in a country where progress is unknown, and where the customs of centuries past still remain, not as traditions but as facts. They were always kind and gentle, and such devoted admirers of our fairer race as to make most admirable nurses for the children, except for their over indulgence.

The towns of Mesilla and Las Cruçes are

as characteristic in their way as any of old Spain, and quite as interesting. We passed through both *en route* to Bayard, and my pen would fain linger over their many peculiarities. Several days elapsed after leaving the Rio Grande before our arrival at Fort Bayard in New Mexico, where we prepared to begin afresh the old story of life in a new garrison. Baby had climbed over me until I was glad to rest on terra firma again.

CHAPTER XV.

FORT BAYARD, surrounded by high mountains, is pleasantly situated in a very hilly region. The officers' quarters face the Santa Rita Mountains, which rise to an abrupt point directly opposite the post, a few miles distant, forming a landmark which is not soon forgotten, especially if constantly in view for three years, during which time we had the good fortune to remain there.

On the brow of that sharp decline, which rises almost at right angles with the hill beneath, a large, irregularly shaped rock had fallen, which bears a perfect resemblance to a kneeling figure, and faces the higher point. It was called the kneeling nun, and, of course, invested with the natives by a suggestive history. The suppliant posture is perfect, and the figure conveyed to me a world of deep meaning.

That little corner of South-western New Mexico, in which we remained three years, a length of sojourn so unusual and unexpected that every spring I looked for an order to move, has an unwritten history which would cover many pages. It is the mining region of New Mexico, and has the most perfect climate of any in the United States, neither extremely warm in summer, nor severely cold in winter; and the sun shines at least three hundred days in each year with a warmth and brightness which render life perfectly enjoyable, if spent out of doors as it should be.

The only real storms are in summer, when during the rainy season clouds suddenly gather in the afternoon, and are followed by such a downpour of rain, with perhaps thunder and lightning, that it seems as if everything would be washed away. After the full force and fury of the elements have been spent, every cloud disappears, and the day ends with a perfect sunset, which is followed by a night still, calm, and wonderfully beautiful.

Occasionally, but not often, snow falls in winter; altogether, the climate is perfect, and I have often since wondered why that locality is not popular as a health resort, for a more bracing and invigorating air is never breathed anywhere.

On account of the infrequency of rain, vegetation is not very green, but neither is it shriveled and parched. Cattle never fail to find succulent pasturage in the bunch grass, which even when perfectly dry is nutritious. But for the constant Indian depredations from which that region has suffered for twenty years, it would be the garden spot of the West. The climate is much milder in winter than that of Colorado.

Mines of every description have been found in New Mexico, from the famous Santa Rita copper mines, which bear traces of having been worked centuries ago, to more recently discovered ones of silver and gold. These latter have caused the building of the only American town, known there, Silver City, which, with its one hundred beautiful red brick houses, is a wonderful place, considering the locality and surroundings. All this is, however, more recent, although the town had a number of fine residences when we were there nearly a score of years ago. It is only an hour's drive from Fort Bayard, over the most lovely rolling mountain road, and the visits to Silver City were a very pleasant feature of our life when at that fort.

The Fort Bayard which first greeted our eyes was, except for climate and scenery, a sorry place. It boasted a large garrison, but we were shown into a perfectly miserable hut that was our shelter for months. The cabins or huts in which the officers lived were directly back of the new quarters, stone foundations for which had already been laid.

The houses were to be built of adobe bricks, that were made by simply mixing to a proper consistency with water the earth obtained from excavating in front of our dwellings, shaping in primitive wooden molds, and drying in the hot sun.

All the workmen were slow-moving Mexicans, who built houses in the same way as had their forefathers for generations. They knew no meaning for the word " hurry," so it took months to erect those simple homes; and meantime we not only lived in wretched huts, but could not venture out after dark for fear of falling into some one of the many pits.

Our experience was dreadful for one long year, then the houses were finally completed. The ground had been so torn up that the least gust of wind seemed sufficient to start all the loose earth in motion, when we would be almost buried in clouds of dust; but our worst trouble was during the rainy season.

Our houses were situated on the brow of a hill, and when sudden summer storms arose they washed right through the house. We preferred to give them the right of way rather than have the buildings, wretched as they were, entirely disappear, so the back doors would be opened, and the storms permitted to sweep through before finding egress at the front doors. The houses, so-called by courtesy, were merely log cabins without floors; it was therefore necessary, at such times, to mount on chairs or tables if we desired to escape mud baths. The roofs, thatched with straw and overlaid with mud, had a way of leaking that was apt to result in huge mud-puddles being spread in all directions. The ladies always took refuge under umbrellas until after the storms subsided.

None could envy others, for all were in the same boat, with no comforts whatever. Sometimes the whole roof fell in, but no one was ever hurt, and on the two occasions which I recall, bachelor officers were the sufferers.

The lieutenant-colonel who commanded our post, having no family, had kindly given his house to a little bride, whose husband was a recent graduate of West Point. She, like myself, had started out expecting to find all military stations like that lovely place, and had brought from New York the most luxurious outfit ever seen on the frontier. Magnificent carpets and curtains from Sloan's, fit for any New York palace, had been shipped all that long distance, and she proceeded to lay the former directly over the mud floor in her house, and to hang the latter at her little windows.

The house was in every respect like all the rest, with three rooms in a row, and one or two forming an ell; yet she had decked the interior to look like a perfect fairy bower. The front room, that opened directly out of doors, was the sitting-room; back of that was a sleeping apartment, and then the kitchen.

When the first severe storm arose and swept right through that house, the rain coming in at the back and going out at the front door, I never saw a more dismayed and discouraged woman than was our little bride, and no wonder. Her fairy bower had been transformed into a mud-bank; the pretty white curtains were streaked and discolored beyond recognition, the carpets covered with mud, while the pictures and ornaments were unrecognizable.

That lady was like many I have met, both before and since. She expected ordinary modes of life to prevail at the frontier, and had carried with her at least a dozen large trunks, for which she was glad to find simply storage, and whose pretty contents never saw the light.

Her experience was pitiable. Having an abundance of money, she naturally supposed it would purchase some comforts ; but money was of no use to her there, and, indeed, seemed only an aggravation. The little woman used to send East for articles, which for economy's sake the rest of us went without, and disappointments invariably followed. Whatever was received — which would be only after almost incredible waiting — was never what she had expected ; and if garments had been ordered, alterations which none but a skilled hand could make were always needed.

I remember being once consulted about a Christmas present designed for her husband. She had decided upon a beautiful picture, which, although ordered in ample time, did not arrive until long after the holidays, and the express charges alone were fifty dollars. Her disappointments were well nigh endless, and led me to believe that money was not so much a promoter of happiness in frontier life as it would usually be considered elsewhere ; for no matter how much people were able to spend they could not buy luxuries, and to send East for them meant only tantalization and weary waiting.

Perhaps some of my own experiences in the matter of express charges may not prove uninteresting. Every woman is said to love a new bonnet ; but army women show the greatest unconcern regarding fashions, probably because their lives are so different from those of their city sisters.

When some head covering became a positive necessity, we usually sent East for a plain little hat, dark and useful, as it was needed mainly for wear when driving around the country. I had quite worn out my Eastern supply after a two years' residence at Bayard, so ordered a quiet little hat or bonnet from New York. Instead, I received a very gaudy, dashing piece of millinery that would have been suitable for the opera, but was altogether out of place on the frontier. The bonnet cost twenty dollars, and the express charges were twenty-two. For that entirely useless arrangement, therefore, I had to pay forty-two dollars, and then had no bonnet, for I never wore it.

That little lady had all the ambition and pride in a refined way of living that naturally arose from having spent her early life amid luxurious surroundings. She had passed several years in the gayest capitals of Europe, had imbibed most extravagant ideas from fond and indulgent parents, had scarcely ever known an ungratified wish, and was therefore less prepared for the actual realities of life, as developed at Fort Bayard, than any one else I have ever known. The desire and attempt to live in accordance with her means resulted in constant disappointments and trials. I have never seen any one who worked so hard to accomplish what were considered simply necessities, and yet whose labor was so entirely unrewarded.

She wanted to entertain lavishly; and having beautiful table appointments it was really a treat to dine at her house; but when she told of the labor involved, by reason of incompetent help, the task seemed too great to include any pleasure. Her utter ignorance of household duties made her an easy prey to servants' wiles, and the very fact that she could so lavishly supply materials only made them more ready to take advantage.

She tried the same experiment we had — taking a servant from New York — but fared even worse, as her maid left when Santa Fé was reached, saying she did "not care to go any farther from civilization." The officer's wife had no redress, although she had spent quite a large sum both on the girl's fare and baggage, as they had traveled by stage.

When, a year later, this same lady had a dear little girl born, she offered, but in vain, fifty dollars a week to any one who would care for herself and child. It was really pitiful to see the beautiful young woman lying neglected, deprived of the most common care, when if money could have availed she would have been enveloped in luxury. Of course, attentions were received from other ladies, but hers was one of the many cases I have known where Dame Nature alone was at hand to assist.

My pen glides lovingly over the paper when I begin to describe army ladies, and fain would linger to fill page after page with loving reminiscences of their sweet goodness and devotion to husbands and the cause they represented. Surely in no other life can women be found who are at once so brave and true.

At each post I formed devoted attachments to some woman, and were the love experienced for them all and their perfections to be described, this book could contain little else; for one story after another of their wifely devotion and absolute self-abnegation, carried to such an extent as to be actually heroic, is recalled.

No murmur was ever heard at the order to move, if women were to be included; for no matter how hard, long, or wearisome the journey, they were content if permitted to accompany their husbands. But when the officers were sent away on the many expeditions cavalry service demanded, where their wives could not go with them, then were they indeed wretched; hours and days seemed endless until the return of loved ones.

This intense devotion was the cause of incessant hardships being borne; for in many instances, if the ladies would have returned to their Eastern homes, care and attention would have been bestowed which can never be expected on the frontier.

The difficulty of obtaining competent help in household cares could never be surmounted. Even when near Mexican settlements we would find that a long line of idle ancestry, together with every tendency of climate, surroundings, and viciousness, had so developed indolence in the natives as to utterly incapacitate them for any serious employment. They were capable only of such tasks as allowed them to bask in the sun and smoke cigarettes all day long. As they made admirable nurses, and we liked to have our children live out of doors, they could be utilized in that way; but heavier household tasks were left for more energetic hands.

When I think of that delicious sun and air, and recall those happy days, I wonder how any thing can be remembered except the absolute content experienced when we finally moved into our new quarters, and regularly settled down into sweet home life. The children throve and bloomed like flowers, and were never ill.

In the South-western climate ordinary diseases do not prevail, and if any of the epidemics which mothers usually dread break out, the absolute pureness of the air renders them innocuous; and with even ordinary care children speedily recover. Army doctors, in the double capacity of physician and family friend, also give most extraordinary care, so sickness is rarely fatal. Except from teething and its attendant ills, babies are almost exempt from maladies, and children live so secluded from outside influences that mine never even had measles or any other childish disease.

One beautiful babe died from teething, and during its illness every lady in the post passed her entire time at its bedside when allowed to do so. But that may be instanced as only one proof of the sincere interest felt in each other by people who are isolated from all the rest of the world.

CHAPTER XVI.

I HAVE always thought army life would be delightful if there was the slightest certainty of remaining at any post for a given length of time ; but this is so out of the question that many comforts which might otherwise be procured are gradually tabooed.

Officers become so accustomed to expect removal, that they are unwilling to accumulate comforts which must be left when marching orders are received; and every one is apt to give credence in some degree to the rumors which continually gain ground, and usually emanate from an unknown source, that a change is soon to be made. One lives in a veritable atmosphere of unrest until it becomes second nature.

At Bayard, for the first time during our army

life, we felt somewhat settled. Cavalry service
consists entirely of unforeseen emergencies, de-
pendent upon the country's condition and its
need for the movement of troops, either in the
pursuit of Indians or horse-thieves. As Mr.
Boyd had been sent to superintend the building
of the quarters at Bayard, we felt that unless
his regiment moved he would remain as quartermaster until they were completed, so quietly
established ourselves in one of the new houses
to enjoy life and a more prolonged stay than
usual.

We made many pleasant friends in the neighboring town of Silver City, enjoyed a great
deal of company from there, and always drove
over to the entertainments they gave, some of
which were of a very comical nature.

Imagine a ball at which every element is represented, from the most refined to the most un-
cultivated, from the transplanted branches of
excellent Eastern families, who lured by enti-
cing descriptions of great mineral wealth to be
found at the West had gone there in search of

fortunes, to the rudest specimens of frontier life, who had never seen anything else, and were devoid of all education, yet, like true Americans, regarded themselves as the very quintessence of knowledge and good-breeding.

The balls were always held in the court-house; and when, during court session, the judge and attendant lawyers were to be honored with an entertainment in consonance with their dignity, the rude room would be cleared of benches just before the hour at which the dance was to begin, and pretty dresses would trail over the floor which had not been cleaned for weeks, and which was the recipient of every kind of *débris*.

At one of those balls, held immediately after court had adjourned, the window-sills had been made receptacles for all such usual appliances of lawyers as paper, pens, and ink. The army-post guests laid their many wraps in one of those windows because there was no dressing-room. In fact, such a luxury was unknown. When ready to return home, our wraps were

pulled down, and with them came several bottles of ink, which sprinkled their contents lib-
erally over shawls and head-gear. As usual, I
was a sufferer, and have to this day, as memento of the occasion, a very handsome shawl
that was completely ruined. But to remain
at home from the only pleasure our circumstances afforded was not to be thought of, and
fine clothes were willingly sacrificed.

We could rarely indulge in dancing-parties
at Bayard because there were so few ladies.
When, occasionally, a special effort in that direction was made, the fact that we had no
proper dancing-hall would be emphasized, and
the large double parlors of our commanding
officer's house utilized. With the facilities at
hand for decorating them with beautiful flags,
cannon, stacked bayonets and swords, we gave
several dances, which contrasted favorably with
the town balls, and quite cured me of any
desire to ever again dance on so different a
floor.

Yet we sincerely enjoyed our Silver City

friends, and our greatest pleasure was to drive over and visit them, returning early in the evening, very much fatigued, but happy because we lived near any sort of town, instead of being cut entirely off from all outside life.

Our cook often rebelled at the large parties of friends who sometimes visited us unexpectedly, and, as before in similar experiences, showed his displeasure by indulging too freely in " strong water." One day he notably distinguished himself, and almost extinguished me, by reeling in before a whole party of friends who were awaiting luncheon, and declaring that he was no slave, neither had he engaged himself as a hotel cook. His freedom of manner was so natural among frontier people, that every one laughed, and all sallied out in the dining-room, where we passed around bowls of bread and milk.

We had two excellent cows, and my delight was to work large rolls of butter into dainty pats for the table. Never before or since have I so enjoyed housekeeping as at Fort Bayard. Our chickens seemed fairly to multiply, and I could keep no count of the eggs they laid. We were able to supply every one, and still have quantities left for our own use.

I was in my element; for I found that by dint of judicious management fifty dollars a month could be laid aside, so in two years' time we were entirely out of debt, and fully resolved never again to enter the state. That was our golden harvest time, and I look back upon it with unspeakable pleasure.

I would like the ability to describe one beautiful friend who was my constant companion at that time, but no pen can do justice to the admirable traits of so perfect a woman. She is still with her husband in the West, a pattern of all womanly goodness. Her example may well be followed by all who leave good homes to follow their husbands in army life, for only the absolute unselfishness she so beautifully exemplified will enable women to endure the same hardships. It was her sweet little first baby to whose death I have alluded, and which left us all sincere mourners for her dear sake. She always reminded me of the virtuous woman described in the Bible, whose " children arise up, and call her blessed."

But I must not linger over those recollections of dear Fort Bayard, where we enjoyed a real home for three years, and even flowers in abundance. If people in civil life could know of the weeks and months of care one little plant has often received from an army woman, because a dear reminder of her distant home, they would understand what a luxury it was to be able to raise flowers without any particular effort. Though one loves work, yet it is pleasant to be sometimes rewarded ; and we had never before been where flowers could be freely indulged in, nor have we since.

There was another especial pleasure we enjoyed at Fort Bayard, which to me is the chief charm of army life — constant rides on horseback. At that post they were delightful ; for, go where we would in any direction, excellent mountain roads and superb scenery rewarded us. Our favorite jaunt was to the Santa Rita mountains. Having gained them, we would dismount and explore the famous mines which were tunneled in so many directions that I always feared lest we should be buried alive. Those tunnels had been dug centuries before, and the then so-called "new industry" was but a revival of past labors.

Mr. Boyd, true to his nature, which was to employ every moment in devoted service to the government, rarely found time to escort me until after the day's duties were over; or we would arise very early in the morning, and enjoy a ride that colored my mind for weeks with a vague fancy that life was not altogether and entirely real and practical, but was full of deep beauty; and if we could only live more out-of-doors, and be permeated more often and thoroughly with the charms of nature as seen in the early freshness and beauty of such mornings as were those, we should be elevated, and enabled to grasp more of spiritual things than tame and ordinary humdrum life permits.

Oh, I envy the woodsman who is content with nature, and never pines for the artificial life of cities! Nature is perfect, and in such deep solitudes the most prosaic minds must realize this truth.

CHAPTER XVII.

I HAVE not very often referred in this volume to the character of my husband, for in my opinion it needs no vindication. Mr. Boyd always left in the minds of every one with whom he came in contact the impress of a most noble nature. His devotion to duty was so extreme that all else was laid aside at its call; and at Fort Bayard he so entirely gave his whole time and attention to arduous and unremitting labors as to scarcely find time for any pleasures. Mr. Boyd was as much of a worker as ever can be found in civil life, where a man expects reward for faithful service. In the army there is none. Of course that is well understood, and any one who devotes his life to duty there, does it purely from principle.

Two singular occurrences, which have always

been mysteries to me, happened at Fort Bayard. We moved into the new quarters before our new house — a double one — was entirely completed. The part in which we lived was separated from the other by a wall that divided the halls, and the unoccupied side was filled with shavings and *débris.* One night after we had retired, some one laid a lighted candle on a large pile of shavings, which of course caught fire, and we were awakened from sound sleep by a strong smell of smoke. This was soon traced to its source, and we found a fine fire rapidly developing. The floor had burned away, leaving a cavernous depth beneath.

It was unquestionably the work of an incendiary; and a few weeks afterward the same wicked hand, presumably, fired a huge stack of hay, consisting of the entire winter's supply of six hundred tons, which at frontier posts is always stacked near the corral and guarded day and night by sentries.

In that absolutely dry climate such a fire, when once started, has no hindrance to its progress ; and though every available hand was quickly on the spot pouring water, of course it was a useless task. Though a beautiful sight to see that brilliant blaze of light defined against the clear, dark sky, my heart ached when I thought of the trouble and worry it would cause Mr. Boyd, and also of the animals' deprivation. The entire summer had been required in which to procure enough hay for so many; and the fire occurred in early winter, when no more could be cut.

It is a custom in the army at the slightest alarm of fire to sound a call, which brings every man to the spot with a bucket in his hand. It is really marvelous to see how soon ordinary fires yield to army treatment. But if a high wind is blowing, the supply of water, limited to barrels which are placed between the houses and always kept filled, is insufficient, and little can be done to stay -its devastating progress. In spite of sympathy and real concern for losses sustained, one is sure to enjoy the excitement.

I witnessed one shocking fire at Bayard which

broke out in a small private stable attached to
the post-trader's house. It had made such head-
way that when discovered three beautiful horses
were already enveloped in flames : they were
fairly roasted alive before the eyes of the assembled garrison. Most pathetic cries proceeded
from the helpless animals before death merci-
fully released them from their sufferings.

While the ladies sorrowfully looked on, the
men spread wet blankets over an adjoining roof
in order that it might be saved ; for if a tiny
spark had fallen on the dry shingles they would
have immediately ignited and the flames spread
rapidly

After three happy years had been passed at
that post, orders were received to march into
Texas and exchange with the Ninth Cavalry.

Christmas Day was celebrated in camp, and in
a double sense, for we had that morning a nar-
row escape from almost instant death.

On reaching the Rio Grande, we found the
river fairly booming. It was a glorious sight,
swelled to a huge flood that swept past in majes-

tic grandeur. A primitive flat-boat worked by ropes and pulleys — nothing but a rude raft with no railing or chain either fore or aft — was called into requisition to ferry us across, and we sat quietly in the ambulance while it was driven aboard.

A superb dog that belonged to one of our friends, and had been our pet for years, was inadvertently left standing on the bank. Some one on the boat tried to induce him to swim across, making the same sound in calling the dog that would have been used to start the mules. Our four mules, supposing it was a signal to them, immediately started, and the leaders' fore feet were actually on the very edge of the boat when a man seized them by their heads. Another second, another step, and our heavy ambulance would have been overboard.

So rapidly had the occurrence passed that almost before realizing an accident was seemingly inevitable, we had been saved from a watery grave. The river at that point was at least twenty feet deep, and had the mules plunged in, sudden and swift death would have followed.

I have never since been able to sit quietly in a carriage while crossing a ferry; though of course no such rude craft, without even a rope guard, can be found in civilized parts of the world.

After all was over, I looked at my little children, so unconscious of danger, and shuddered at the thought of the horrible fate we had escaped. If people should dwell continually on the perils of Western life they would be wretched. That journey embraced every element of danger, and yet I actually became callous.

Our mules were such superb animals, and so capable of swift progress, that every few days they evinced a spirit with which I heartily sympathized, running for miles and creating a profound excitement throughout the entire command. As nine-tenths of Texas is flat prairie with excellent roads, I rather enjoyed the sensation. Nothing in my whole army experience wearied me so much as those endless days of slow, monotonous travel. When with troops we could not go faster than a walk, for the horses must be favored in order that their strength might hold out during the weeks those journeys consumed; and it was not safe, in the then unsettled condition of the country, for us to ride far in advance.

Our march occupied eight weeks; but some of the troops that were ordered from Northern New Mexico to Southern Texas were between three and four months on the road, and the chapter of incidents which beset their path was remarkable. I have before alluded to this journey — the one on which nine infants were born *en route;* and in every instance mothers and children were obliged to proceed the next day, regardless of health or even life.

During one week of our march it rained day and night, and tents were pitched in the midst of mud and general discomfort; but after a cheerful blaze had been started in our little stove we did not mind so very much, though of course it was not pleasant. The real trials from which others suffered, and which were therefore kept constantly in mind, enabled us to realize that our lot might be much worse.

The baggage of one woman, who had four little girls to clothe and care for, was deluged in crossing the Pecos River, and the fact not discovered until their destination had been reached, when the clothes dropped in pieces on being touched.

As each family packed all superfluities, and kept only a traveling outfit, the trunks with reserve clothing were never opened while *en route;* and the treacherous streams, that seemed shallow enough in crossing, would often, in some inexplicable way, reach the contents of the wagons.

To me the strangest part of that journey was the passing over so much territory without seeing any inhabitants. El Paso, then a mining-town of very slight importance, was the last we saw in Texas. If there were others in that section they could not have been on the traveled highway; for except the military posts, we saw nothing but prairies, which were indeed a striking contrast to our beautiful mountains.

We had all sorts of experiences before New Mexico was left; but after that we settled down to calm travel, which the children enjoyed so much, and that was rendered less monotonous to me by the daily use of a fine saddle horse, and a delightful gallop over tufted grass.

We remained at Mesilla and Las Cruçes long enough to enjoy a ball given in our honor by the residents; and there, for the first time, we saw really beautiful Mexican women, who danced with all the grace for which the Spanish race is noted. We were obliged to hasten our departure, because the soldiers celebrated Christmas too freely; during the ball a perfect battle was raging outside, which compelled the officers to break camp and resume the march before daylight, leaving us to follow.

Those old towns of Mesilla and Las Cruçes would surprise any one from the East. They are situated on the Rio Grande, and surrounded by dense and forbidding sand-hills; but the location being such that much irrigation is practicable, are simply the most fruitful imaginable places.   I have never anywhere else seen such absolute abundance of fruit in its season; grapes such as only a southern sun can ripen, and in immense clusters; peaches, large and luscious, that loaded the trees till it seemed impossible they could bear the burden and live; apricots, and every species of small fruits.   The same luxuriance prevails in El Paso, and the wine made there is pure and delicious.

It seems needless to dwell at very great length on that journey into Texas, for all those marches were so monotonously alike.   If, as in that case, no Indian dangers were to be feared, both on account of our cavalry escort, and because at that time no active Indian warfare was in progress, we were not allowed to forget the possibilities in that line.   Not only were the usual sad reminders present in graves that bestrewed the country, but we encamped again and again in places where the most violent outrages had been perpetrated, and entire parties mercilessly slaughtered. It cast a sad shadow over our resting-places, which shrinking women would fain have escaped; but we were obliged to use the same old accustomed grounds, and even then could not always find enough water for the horses and mules.

That journey was on a progressive scale; and guided by previous experiences we had taken two wall tents, and even a board floor for the outer one in which we dined. It was quite envied by other ladies, particularly when we had ten consecutive days of rain; for boards, even if laid on wet ground inside a tent, make a flooring quite different and much superior to mud. Our floor was, of course, in sections, otherwise it could not have been carried. Skins covered the earth in our inner tent, which was furnished with two large beds.

A fire was lighted every night in our tiny stove, and I made chocolate, custards, and many other dainties. It would surprise Eastern people, who deem all the modern conveniences a necessity, to see how systematic even such a mode of life can be, when, knowing it is to last for weeks and months, proper preparations have been made.

On leaving home we had taken the house-keeping supplies that would have been used had we remained stationary. So, when encamped in different military posts, at which we always remained several days, I occupied the time in making mince-pies and baking them in a Dutch oven, which is nothing more nor less than a broad and shallow iron pot, with a cover like a frying-pan. On this cover hot coals are laid, so when the utensil is placed over a bed of the same, uniform heat from above and beneath bakes admirably.

It was a time of rejoicing when we could remain long enough at a post to straighten out the tangled ends continuous travel always produces. Journeying in that way with women and children necessitated laundry work; and when we encamped on the river bank the scene was animated.

Again our route lay for days beside the Rio Grande; in fact, during our entire journey we left it only to make a *détour* and return. When finally our destination, distant Fort Clark, was reached, we were but forty miles from that famous river, and nearly the entire regiment was to find a resting-place on its banks; for soon our encampments were dispersed from Eagle Pass, on the river, to Matamoras, six hundred miles below, at its mouth.

We heard so many wearisome accounts of those lower camps, with their continuous heat and glare, as to deem ourselves fortunate in being permitted to remain at one situated on a high hill, where we would be sure of a breeze, however warm the Texas summer nights might prove.

A large ball was given on our arrival, and the different posts at which we had stopped *en route* — Forts Bliss, Davis, and Stockton — had all honored us in the same way.

We were obliged to remain in camp at Fort Clark ten days, as the Ninth Cavalry did not leave sooner for New Mexico, and consequently houses were not vacated. Never did the same length of time seem longer or more tedious, the shelter of a roof once again was so longed for. Finally we moved into a very comfortable little house, built of limestone, and charming as to exterior; for even in the month of February vines were growing rapidly, and beginning to cover verandas with beautiful green.

If each woman who has lived at Fort Clark would give a chapter of her experiences while there, I know people would be interested because of the utter novelty.

No other army post has ever been the scene of so constant a succession of regimental changes, and at no other have such a large number of people, for the same reason, been made so uncomfortable. However little there might have been to expect in all the other territories in which we had lived, that little, when once obtained, was kept; but at Clark no one seemed sure, from day to day, of any house in which he lived remaining his own for a length of time.

This arose partly from the fact of there being an insufficient number of quarters, but mainly from the position of the post being such that troops were sent there to be held in readiness for any emergency — which was generally supposed to be impending war with Mexico.

We were so near the border that whenever any marauding band of Indians or horse-thieves succeeded in capturing a herd of cattle from some neighboring ranch, they would coolly slip over the Rio Grande into Mexico with their booty; and by the time our troops, again and again called out, could overtake them, the marauders would have crossed the border, where capture was impossible, because Mexico allowed no American forces to enter her territory without special permission.

Matters continued on that basis for years, infuriating our troops, who were delighted when it produced results that seemed likely to culminate in a war between the two countries.

But that never occurred, though its threatenings filled our post with troops until they formed

a little army, which when mustered in full
parade stretched in double columns across the
immense parade ground, and made a beautiful
sight; one which, seen daily, was so pleasing
that we almost forgot the discomforts of life
that surrounded us.

Our first home, a pretty little house with
double parlors on the ground floor and two large
bedrooms above, seemed delightful; though we
had no furnishings for months, and simply
used our camp equipage, until carpets, etc.,
could be sent for. The climate was so fearfully
hot, bare floors were no hardship; and during
the long summer which followed our arrival, I
was so absorbed in the problem of how to live
at all, that the absence of luxuries was un-
heeded.

Leaving the bright and bracing climate of
New Mexico for a country where one hundred
and ten degrees in the shade was only to be expected, and for six months of the year, was indeed a transition. Ice was an unknown luxury.
We had nothing to use for cooling purposes

except the *ollas*, made of porous earth by Mexicans.

The post was one hundred and thirty-five miles from San Antonio, the nearest point where anything except absolute essentials could be obtained ; and as stages were the only means of transportation, charges of course were exorbitant.   Even in San Antonio there was none but manufactured ice ; and to transport it such a distance in so warm a climate, required not only much sawdust to prevent its melting, but also a heavy box, all of which multiplied its weight, and the express charges, as I found to my sorrow.

I never indulged in such luxuries ; but an officer, who considered himself indebted for kindnesses extended during a severe attack of malarial fever, was most anxious to show his gratitude ; and when I, in turn, succumbed to the fever, that was epidemic, he sent me three boxes of ice.   I accepted the gift, though, not caring for the ice, dispatched it to the hospital. Some months afterward we received a bill from the express office which amounted to eighteen dollars. It was the charges on that ice — which we paid. The ice having been sent direct to us, so was the bill, instead of being presented to our kind friend who never imagined the sequel.

After our bountiful supply of good things in Bayard, we nearly starved in Texas. The butter was simply oil, if procurable at all; the milk thin — not tasteless, but with a decidedly disagreeable flavor of wild garlic and onions; and the beef dry, and with so strange a flavor we could not eat it. Vegetables could not be procured; and potatoes shipped from a distance were a mass of decay when received. I never knew a woman who, amid all those conditions of improper and insufficient food and severe heat, did not lose health and strength.

For two years I re-lived all my former experiences in trying to keep house under every disadvantage.

We had hoped much from the accounts of famous colored cooks, who, in our experience, proved delusions and snares. We had a succession so worthless that I never have overcome my prejudice against them. They must have been field-hands, who trusting to our Northern ignorance boldly announced themselves as cooks, when perhaps they had never cooked even one simple meal before. Each was succeeded by a worse specimen, until finally, in despair, I begged for a soldier. After that, housekeeping became once again a pleasure, even if under difficulties; for I had a willing coadjutor, who joined heartily in my plans to disguise the flavor of meats by every art we could devise in the way of seasoning.

When the long, hot summer had worn its weary six months away, we began to again breathe freely, and with the advent of cooler weather found ourselves able to enjoy every pleasure. The heat had been so intense that during its continuance life had been simply endured. Then everything brightened and improved, as it always does with custom or habit; or rather, we knew better how to overcome dif-

ficulties as time and experience familiarized us
with them.

In the winter we not only had better beef,
because of the grass which had grown during
summer, so the cattle were not obliged to eat
weeds and vegetables, but, for the same reason,
our milk improved in flavor; butter also kept
its consistency.

The experience of a little bride on whom I
called one summer evening will perhaps better
illustrate the difficulties of housekeeping. In
reply to my inquiry if she did not find the enforced idleness because of heat tiresome, she
said :

" I am never idle, because my entire time is
occupied in keeping wet clothes around the
jars that contain our milk and butter."

In that atmosphere of heat, devoid of damp-
ness, no sooner was a wet cloth wrapped about
a jar than it began to dry, and evaporation
cooled the contents. If in addition the jar
was placed in a draught, great results in that
line were attained, but at the expense of constant attention.

One reason that made our army life endurable was the constant exchange of grievances, and our real sympathy one for the other. A group of ladies would naturally fall into conversation regarding the peculiar trials of such a life, and yet not one of them could have been persuaded to leave her husband and seek more comfortable and civilized surroundings.

Fort Clark eventually became very dear to me; but the first two years were exceedingly trying, for I had to accustom myself anew to fresh modes in every direction. The peculiarities of our colored servants would fill a volume.

CHAPTER XVIII.

It took our first colored cook, a huge, strapping creature, who seemed a very giant in strength and stature, three days to scrub our tiny kitchen floor; and his ideas, one of which was that he should sleep until nine o'clock in the morning, nor did he awaken then unless called, were not to be changed to suit our convenience.

I remember so well our first breakfast! Rice batter cakes had been ordered; but the strangest looking and queerest tasting dish was produced, which, when questioned, the cook admitted was simply rice and molasses mixed together and fried in much grease.

Our last colored cook was so surly I was afraid of him, and rejoiced when he was finally replaced by a white man. On leaving us he moved to the little town of Brackett, and after only a few days had passed, murdered a woman, and to hide his guilt burned the house. Circumstantial evidence was so-strong that he was captured and imprisoned in the little jail, which, constructed of heavy stone, was the only decent building in town. The murdered woman had been the widow of a white soldier, and his comrades-in-arms determined to avenge her. So, one night, under cover of the darkness, a number stormed the jail. Though well guarded, and the thick doors seemingly impregnable, they effected an entrance.

Meantime the garrison was greatly alarmed, for the town was so near we could hear the firing and tumult. The ladies were doubly frightened, because each one's husband had been summoned to march at the head of his troops and quell the disturbance.

All were terrified, scarcely knowing what had happened, and the volume of sound that reached our ears made us dread untold dangers. We were frightened at having been left alone, and more alarmed for our husbands, because, in the promiscuous firing which began the moment the troops reached town, we knew not what shot had or might hit one of them.

Altogether we were panic-stricken, and moments seemed hours until the troops returned, which they did very soon, and without a single officer or soldier having been injured, although the shots were numerous enough to have killed an army.

The jail had been forced before the arrival of the troops; but the soldiers, though carefully searching every cell, had been unable to find the prisoner, and, after vowing vengeance on the authorities for having removed him, assembled outside, where they vented their wrath and disappointment by firing against the heavy stone building. When the cavalry reached the scene, and in their turn began to fire, every man disappeared, escaping under cover of the darkness and confusion, and found his way back to the fort, where at roll-call all answered to their names as innocently as possible.

The officers were inclined to condone the offense, both from sympathy with the murdered woman's friends, and also because the murderer was such a despicable coward, as was proved not only by his taking a woman's life, but also in his behavior afterward.

The first officer who entered the jail was Mr. Boyd, who was at once told by the sheriff that the murderer was secreted on its roof, which, unknown to outsiders, had a stone coping six feet high that well concealed him. A more pitiable object was never seen; for expecting every moment would be his last he was praying and groaning in true darkey fashion, and had the tumult outside been less would have been quickly discovered.

Mr. Boyd tried to calm him, but it was useless; the man was so thoroughly frightened he could not be silenced, but kept calling on the good Lord for protection, and throwing himself about with the most grotesque contortions of face and figure.

The sequel proved the soldiers to have been

right in not trusting to the course of law, for
in Texas no crime but that of horse-stealing is
considered deserving of hanging; the murderer
was only imprisoned, but fortunately for himself was taken to another county.

On this occasion Mr. Boyd interviewed a
murderer to whose tender mercies his own
family had been exposed, and after that I was
allowed to have a white cook; for although
they sometimes indulged in dissipation, colored
men and women did the same, and there is no
such fear known on earth as that a woman
experiences when confronted by a drunken
negro.

The cavalry stationed at Fort Clark previous
to our arrival had been colored, though the
infantry, which composed half the post, was
white.

Never having been South before, we had much
to learn before a home feeling was possible.
The level country seemed strange after having
lived among lovely mountains, and we had a
new set of insects to deal with. I had thought

nothing could be worse than my first enemies, the wasps, but soon found the immense roaches with which our house was actually crammed much more disagreeable. They not only covered the kitchen floor until it was black, but actually flew around our heads, and even invaded the bedrooms up-stairs until life seemed intolerable. A thorough system of cleaning and scrubbing was instituted; for they love dirt, which was, in fact, the original cause of such an undue supply. We tried borax and all other known remedies, and in time greatly lessened their numbers.

A picnic in Texas was simply impossible on account of the red bugs and wood-ticks, which were not only countless and disagreeable, but so poisonous that I knew an officer, who had been obliged to camp out on the ground, suffer so severely from their attentions that hospital treatment was necessary for weeks. The sores caused by these insects are frequently very painful, because they bury themselves beneath the skin, and actually have to be dug out.

The larger vermin, scorpions, tarantulas, centipeds, and snakes I did not mind; for they
never molested us, and, like the really weighty
trials of life, were more easily endured than
minor ones. I speak from actual experience,
having lived out of doors during our five years
residence in Texas, and allowed my children to
enjoy themselves in the same way, both because
I deemed it necessary to health, and because
observation had convinced me that those ladies
who did otherwise suffered indescribably from
fear; while to us, after we had settled down,
every moment was a joy in spite of heat and
vermin.

One evening a lady caller started franti-
cally for the door immediately after having
entered. The cause of her terror was a huge
tarantula or spider of the most deadly sort,
black, ugly, and venomous, which measured
fully three inches around the body. I picked
up a heavy basket and killed it. She called
me very brave; but I thought greater bravery
would have been required to permit it to live,

when perhaps it might bite one of my children.

Our first winter at Fort Clark was delightful. All had comfortable double houses; and I felt very proud because of the bright, pretty carpets and lace curtains that had been sent from the East. The troops were called out only occasionally for Indian raids, but never went farther than the river which divides Texas from Mexico.

We enjoyed the game, which was so plentiful that delicious wild turkey could be enjoyed every day if desired. The one vegetable that grew almost spontaneously was sweet potato, which we luxuriated in for months, as it improved by keeping.

I scoured the country on horseback in all directions, and found a rare charm in those boundless prairies, carpeted with gray grass so thick the horse's hoofs sank far out of sight, which made the pace an exhilarating bound. A stream, which rose from the clear spring that supplied us with water, flowed for miles amid groves of wild oak and pecan trees which it was my delight to explore.

We hunted jack rabbits a good deal. They were so numerous as to destroy all hopes of the gardens in which the early freshets had allowed us to indulge. A lady just from the East was appalled when I said that each small head of cabbage cost a dollar, and was really worth it; for the man who had sufficient enterprise to evade rabbits, and build walls against freshets, must also examine each cabbage leaf three times a day in order to destroy the ever encroaching worm or bug. This will not seem exaggerated to any one who has ever gardened under similar conditions.

Our little streams were beautiful, and so well stocked with delicious bass and trout that the children used to beg to picnic: after a day thus spent, it would take hours of diligent search to find the dozens of wood-ticks and tiny red insects which covered their clothing and buried themselves in their tender flesh. Sometimes one would escape notice, and be afterward found with head imbedded beneath the skin, and body distended to treble its original size.

Those torments made scouting in Texas a thing to be dreaded; and yet, after the first year of quiet, our cavalry were kept in the field nine months out of twelve. Though encamped most of the time on the banks of a stream only seven miles distant, yet none the less they were separated from us, and as the officers' wives said, "Compelled us to keep up two messes, and incur great expense, besides being lonely and forlorn."

The sun's scorching heat made it impossible to raise any flowers, for if plants grew and budded the fierce heat would burn the outer petals so blossoms never fully opened. Only one plant, the Madeira vine, throve there, and it was esteemed a special luxury; for as the post was located on a high limestone ridge, and the houses were built of limestone, the white glare was something to be dreaded. Those luxuriant green vines covered our porches so closely as to form perfect little arbors, and enabled us to enjoy out-of-door life. At least two hammocks were swung on every veranda, and they were occupied most of the time, for the air was so hot and lifeless that effort was impossible.

Only one of the five summers we passed at Fort Clark was cool and comfortable. That year the rainy season commenced late and lasted throughout the summer. The other four were so fearfully hot and uncomfortable that we were much exhausted when cooler weather arrived.

Nevertheless, strange as it may seem, after we had once become accustomed to the life and that routine which alone makes existence in warm countries endurable, we were satisfied.

During the day our costumes were the lightest and airiest that could be devised. But when evening came — and no woman ever ventured out-of-doors until after sunset — we arrayed ourselves in pretty white dresses, and started forth to enjoy the breeze, whose never-failing, grateful presence was compensation for the day's intense heat.

In that clear atmosphere the tiniest arc of a moon gives more light than does a full one under other conditions; so by the time its greatest splendor was reached, nothing on earth could have surpassed the perfect beauty of those southern nights. The air was soft and balmy, and every one rejoiced to find respite from the sun's extreme heat. Indeed, the change was so grateful that we fell into a habit of almost turning night into day in our unwillingness to leave a scene of such enchantment.

Even our unsheltered, gray parade-ground, on which grass absolutely refused to grow, was softened by the moon's mellow rays into a semblance of all we desired it to be; and when, night after night, our glorious band played entrancing strains of sweet music on the luminous spot, we felt that life in the tropics was not so very unendurable after all.

Our limestone houses, which in the daytime could not be looked upon because of the blinding glare, were toned by the moon's magic influence into poetic beauty, with their shading vines and groups of dainty ladies in white, and gallant officers in uniform.

I became wedded, heart and soul, to that part of our life, which made me quite willing to live and die in Texas, despite many more prosaic drawbacks.

CHAPTER XIX.

THAT unpleasant features were there is not, however, to be denied; and as my aim is to present both the lights and shadows of army life, I will now describe a few of the latter.

As before stated, the supposed impending war with Mexico was the occasion of an influx of troops far greater than our post could comfortably accommodate. After we had been at Fort Clark a year and a half, occupying that pretty, vine-embowered house, we learned that our garrison of ten companies was to be increased to twenty-five, with two headquarters and two bands.

The custom that obtains throughout the army of each officer selecting according to his rank the quarters which he may prefer, was never more fully enforced than at Fort Clark.

Fifty times, perhaps, there was a general move of at least ten families, because some officer had arrived who, in selecting a house, caused a dozen other officers to move, for each in turn chose the one then occupied by the next lower in rank. We used to call it "bricks falling," because each toppled that next in order over; but the annoyance was endured with great good nature.

When tidings of such an unusual expected influx reached our ears, we wondered what would become of us, as there were not accommodations for half the number who were to arrive. An onlooker would doubtless have found the anxiety experienced by the officers' wives amusing; for though prepared for the worst we were, of course, solicitous.

I was ill at the time, confined to my room; and messages were brought at intervals from six different officers, who all outranked Mr. Boyd, that each had selected our house. Ridiculous as it may seem, every one was outranked by another. Finally, a captain of infantry chose our quarters, and then the doctor declared I could not be moved; consequently, the captain went temporarily into the house which we were eventually compelled to occupy.

Next day our third child and second son was born. During the entire time of my recovery I indulged a delusive hope that the officer who had chosen our home would be content to remain in the little house he was then occupying, and which I dreaded to think of living in because it was so small for our increased family. Delusive hope! built entirely upon my belief in, or knowledge of, our respective needs. I felt that a bachelor could live less inconveniently in one room than could a family of five.

The very day our baby was born the little fellow contracted whooping-cough from his sister, who, charmed to welcome a new brother, had repeatedly kissed him. I had no idea such a disease was in the garrison, and when we learned of it the harm had been done. Not only did all three of our children suffer in the most pronounced fashion, but it was pitiable to see and hear that tiny baby coughing violently before he was two weeks old. He would turn so black in the face, perhaps a hundred times a day, that his nurse hardly dared close her eyes, as it would be necessary to raise the infant to a perfectly erect posture to prevent his strangling.

In spite of baby's sufferings he never lost flesh, which the doctor said was marvelous, for my neighbors declared they could hear him cough a hundred yards away. Our anxiety was great, and Mr. Boyd was a veritable slave.

For a week I was at death's door with fever; and yet the very day baby was four weeks old we were obliged to move, that the captain, who demanded his house without further delay, might be accommodated. Each of the children caught cold, and bronchitis was added to whooping-cough; in consequence of which, during that and the succeeding winter, I always slept with one hand under baby's head, in order to raise him suddenly when attacked by those terrible fits of coughing.

When I state that our new house consisted of but one room, with a tiny addition back which was quite uninhabitable, and that we lived in such quarters for two long summers and winters, it will scarcely be believed. But even those meager accommodations were not deemed a very severe hardship by many of the ladies who had been at Fort Clark for years before the new quarters had been built, and who told tales of far greater crowding.

Among others, the case of a little bride was cited, who, coming from a luxurious Eastern home, had been glad to find quarters in a hall-way between two other families. One morning her husband was told that some superior officer wanted his hall, and disgusted he resigned.

The recital of many such absolutely true tales might, perhaps, have comforted me in some measure, had we not already endured ten long years of hardships; and it seemed as if the time should have come when length of service counted for something.

But it never does in the army, as possibly

only those know who have realized the fact through actual experience. There one must endure all discomforts as uncomplainingly as possible, and meekly relinquish the refinements of life, which such a mode of living absolutely forbids. For a family of five to live in one room through two fearfully warm summers and two winters was far from pleasant; and in order to relieve ourselves of discomforts so far as was possible, we remained out-doors on our pleasant porch nearly all the time.

The winters were delightful in that part of Texas, and yet very trying. The only really cold weather there is caused by the "northers," which come up so suddenly as to render it out of the question to be prepared for the change. A norther is always preceded by a very sultry day; then the thermometer falls perhaps fifty degrees in an hour, and there is something in the chill north wind which seems to freeze the very blood in one's veins. When, in addition, a rainstorm follows, it is little wonder that the cattle interests of Texas suffer, for no living creature can well exist in such an atmosphere when exposed.

Our little back room faced the north, so we could not use it in winter, for the tiny house, built of wood with a canvas ceiling, was then like a barn ; and it was so old that in summer the canvas and woodwork harbored every species of vermin, with which it simply became alive.

I was awakened one night by the raging of a violent storm that seemed to shake the house to its foundations. The rain descended with such force that I expected every moment the roof would fall in. A glance showed me water pouring in under the door which separated the small back room from the larger one in which we slept. I quickly arose and stepped into the little room to find myself literally wading in water which reached above my ankles. The fierce storm had beaten in the old, weather-worn roof, and through a large hole which had been forced in the canvas ceiling a stream of liquid mud was pouring that deluged everything.

The opening was directly over an open bureau drawer, the contents of which were a strange sight. The mud was formed by rain falling on the accumulation of dirt that miserable old canvas held; and before the storm had ceased our possessions were worthless, and the room, which within our knowledge never had been worthy of the name, was still less so.

Every house in the post was in a wretched condition long before morning, and each woman thought that her individual experience could not be exceeded in misery.

It was so common for roofs to leak and plaster to fall that we expected such mishaps; but fortunately, because they left more serious trouble in their wake, such furious storms were not frequent. One lady, a bride, who until that night had seen only the bright side of army life, decided that if such experiences were common she did not care to become accustomed to them; so one result in that instance was her husband's resignation from the army.

A large double bed stood in one corner of our

only room, and in the other a lounge that could be used for the children at night. Over our bed I swung a hammock, which served admirably for baby's cradle, and as an economy of space it was a great success. But during warm weather the porch, as already stated, was our dwelling-place, and at night the hammock suspended there was frequently occupied by Mr. Boyd; for in such a climate to sleep with four other persons in one small room was not very refreshing.

We were, however, very gay through all our miseries and deprivations; for with seventy-five officers and forty ladies in the garrison many pleasures could be enjoyed. During the first winter we had a series of balls for the exchange of regimental courtesies. Those already stationed at Fort Clark gave a large ball to welcome the new-comers, even if they did turn us out of houses and homes, which courtesy was returned by a very grand affair. Then each regiment — six were represented, two of them colored — extended hospitalities on its individual

account, and each vied with the others in somewhat varying the character of the entertainment.

Following that, the bachelors gave a large
german where the favors were superb. Then
the ladies united in a New Year's reception,
which was said to surpass all the rest. Afterward we had weekly hops, a masquerade and
phantom party, at which it was difficult to hide
our identity; for in a garrison where every personal trait was necessarily observed, to disguise
one's individuality was not easy. Probably the
officer who entered the room encased in a well-
stuffed mattress did so most effectually.

Studying how to puzzle the rest was great
fun. So many amusements, combined with the
real kindly feeling constantly evinced, made our
social life very enjoyable. Every excuse for
pleasant intercourse was freely sought; and so
long as life lasts I shall remember those years
at Fort Clark as not only joyous, but given up
to experiences so distinctly different from all
others as to merit perpetual and delightful
recollection.

In the first place, every one lived out-of-doors nine months of the year. That necessitated, or made more easily possible, a constant interchange of friendly remarks, and we became more like one large family than like strangers. Our interests were identical. If any change was made, it affected so many that all were drawn together by that " fellow feeling which makes us wondrous kind."

When troops were ordered away, their departure was dreaded because the officers' society would be greatly missed. If new-comers arrived, as they constantly did, we welcomed them cordially. Every time an inspecting officer or one of high rank came to Fort Clark, as frequently happened, we rejoiced in the opportunity to give a ball in his honor, and the band serenaded him each night of his sojourn ; in fact, nothing was lacking that would prove our hospitality and cordiality.

Riding and driving parties were indulged in daily ; for fully half of the officers stationed at our garrison were in the cavalry, and in addi-

tion to their mounts had fine carriages. When
the cavalry were sent to graze their horses near
streams, and permanent camps were thus established, we visited them frequently. In turn,
they combined their forces and gave grand
picnics, which were so successful we were en-
raptured.

One night I shall never forget. The moon
shone her best and brightest on a smooth stretch
of canvas, spread so as to form a splendid dan-
cing-floor, and on trees hung with fairy lanterns,
which extending as far as the eye could reach
met as background the pretty little stream on
whose banks lovers wandered. Of course, in
that region of soft tropic warmth and fervor,
romance blended with everything; and no eli-
gible young lady was ever known to leave Fort
Clark without a tiny circlet on her finger,
which proved her right to return as an officer's
bride.

Meantime, rumors of war kept increasing,
and finally all our troops were marched into Mexico during the hottest month of the year. This

was, however, done merely as a menace; for in a week's time they returned, having faced the Mexicans on their own ground without even exchanging shots. Blistered feet and swollen limbs, gained by marching through parching sands, were the only reminders of the affair brought back.

Soon after, Mexico arranged new terms with our authorities, in accordance with which incursions over the border were allowed when our troops were on the trail of desperate adventurers who were escaping with much booty. This caused the withdrawal from Fort Clark of the gallant cavalry regiment, which with our own had hoped to reap a little glory from the strained relations between our country and her sister republic.

Courtesies were exchanged between leading officers in the Mexican and American armies, which we shared in by giving a grand ball to the general and staff of the Mexican army on their visit to our post while negotiating terms of peace. Our third winter at Fort Clark was brilliant socially. We organized a theatrical company, which gave with great success a number of popular plays, including "Caste," "Ours," and several farces that were a source of much merriment. The soldiers were allowed to fill the hall to its utmost capacity, and their appreciation was an additional reward for our efforts.

I doubt if anything can be funnier than a familiar face and form rendered unrecognizable by an absurd and ridiculous disguise. The night "Caste" was produced, I excelled myself in so completely changing Mr. Boyd's appearance that his entrance on the stage as "Old Eccles" was greeted by loud and long-continued shouts, which ceased only to be again and again renewed. It was the success of the evening. In our sentimental parts Mr. Boyd eclipsed us all, and was the cynosure of all eyes in his maudlin drunkenness.

After having studied the book of directions until I understood how to make my husband look utterly disreputable and unlike himself, I delighted in having him assume various odd characters; for the moment he appeared before an audience, deafening applause invariably greeted him.

We worked as hard to secure the success of our plays as though fortunes had depended upon it, and unhesitatingly robbed our houses of ornaments in order that the stage might present an attractive appearance.

I would not like to be a professional on the boards if it necessitated as much real labor as did our amateur performances. But we soon found that a good paying audience could readily be commanded, and after the first few evenings raised money enough to build a very pretty stage, and completely renovate the only hall in the garrison, which had been used for church, schoolroom, ballroom, and theater for years without any improvements or alterations having been made, and was in sad need of the new floor and ceiling our money supplied.

We also gave performances for several charities. One for the famishing Irish, when we

" Caste " our bread upon the waters, was especially successful; and when at the approach of
Christmas, money was needed for a tree with
which to gladden the hearts of the soldiers' one
hundred little children, we had an immense
audience.

The actors afterwards went to San Antonio,
where they played for the Masonic fund; and
also to a little near-by town where a church was
greatly needed.

CHAPTER XX.

It was customary for companies of Mr. Boyd's regiment to be sent for six months to garrison the forts on the Rio Grande, which were close by; our turn came when we had been two years at Fort Clark, which we left reluctantly.

No station immediately on the river was ever considered desirable, on account of its unfailing sand and heat; and Fort Duncan, to which we were assigned, had no comfortable houses. It was only forty miles from Fort Clark, and as but two companies of infantry were stationed there, the small garrison was inevitably dull.

Our dwelling consisted of one room in a very dilapidated building. It had been previously used as a store-room, and the barred windows made it seem prison-like.

The kitchen was so far away that a complete circuit of the house was necessary in order to reach it, and the dining-room was a part of the kitchen.

Our sorrows were added to when our beautiful ponies, that had borne us about the country for miles in every direction during our stay at Clark, and which I had confidently expected would relieve the tedium of life at Duncan, were attacked by glanders and ordered shot. In spite, however, of this caution, the contagion spread; and before another month Mr. Boyd's splendid charger, and our other dear little Mexican pony, had also been condemned. Thus we lost four horses within one month, and I would have been in despair had we not found a superb riding-horse in the troop, which proved so safe and reliable that I was often tempted to go far beyond proper limits.

One day, when riding alone, I espied smoke ahead, and idly followed in its direction until I found myself facing a house which I recalled as having been described to me as a den of horse thieves. My mount was superb, but I was nine miles from home and conscious that rest was imperative. I dismounted, led my horse to the house, and asked for water. The man who appeared not only gave me that, but also coffee; and when I related the loss of my ponies, offered to sell me a fine pair very cheap.

I used my eyes to good advantage, not neglecting to notice a ford, directly in front of the door, which could be utilized at a moment's notice for horses to cross into Mexico. But that was none of my affairs, and like all rough frontiersmen mine host of the hour was exceedingly polite. He led up for inspection several pairs of fine ponies. I did not, however, buy any, as I feared the owners might meet me some day and claim their property.

After a brief rest I remounted, and on reaching home found that my absence had been of five hours' duration, and the entire garrison was alarmed.

We remained at Duncan all that winter, and

aside from daily rides our only amusement was a trip across the river into Mexico. The quaint old town of Piedras Negras lay directly opposite Fort Duncan; and the same style of primitive boats as were used in New Mexico, and on one of which we came so near to losing our lives, was there employed to ferry us across. We were able to enjoy everything Piedras Negras afforded in the way of sight-seeing, having arrived just before the yearly *fiesta*, which is the gala time among Mexicans.

The town, like all I saw in Mexico, was built around squares called *plazas*. These were occupied during the *fiesta* as booths for the sale of curiosities, and also for that sport so dear to Mexican hearts — gambling. Any game could be indulged in, from three card monte to roulette; or, if disposed, visitors might partake of Mexican viands, served by bashful señoritas clad in pretty Spanish costumes.

The climax of festivities was, of course, bullfights, when the large amphitheater would be crowded by an excited Mexican audience. Having heard so much of those affairs, we were, of course, eager to see one ; but our curiosity was soon satisfied, for a more tame encounter I never beheld.

The poor bull absolutely refused to fight, and, after having been goaded and prodded by the matador with sharp-pointed spears, gayly ribbon-bedecked, kept turning wistfully toward the door by which he had entered, and every now and then rushed to it, only to be met by more spear pricks, which, though causing his blood to flow, served only to still farther intimidate the poor animal. Finally, amid the shouts of the people, he would be dispatched and re-placed by another, that invariably showed the same want of spirit.

To American on-lookers it seemed a cruel sport, unworthy its historic greatness.

The only delightful features connected with that so-called pastime were the perfect Mexican band and superb drilling of Mexican soldiers, who marched and countermarched for at least an hour without a single order being spoken, they responding merely to a tap of the drum as each new movement was initiated.

The band was superb, and the music so sweet and thrilling we could have listened for hours without weariness. On account of exchanging many hospitalities with the Mexican officers, we enjoyed numerous opportunities of hearing it.

On one occasion the band was brought over to serenade us, and we listened as in a dream to its rendering of various operas and Mexican national airs, played with such expression that all the sentiments they indicated were aroused.

The perfect submission of Mexican soldiers, and the never-ending drilling they received, made them more thorough than our own, who never could have been kept in such slavish subjection. The Mexican soldier is usually born a *peon*, or slave, and never dreams of resenting the will of his superiors — nor of having one of his own.

Those men were drilled hours before dawn, and that they might be in good marching order were compelled to walk ten and even twenty miles a day out in the open country.

We were invited to all balls given by the Mexican officers, and found them curious affairs. The women's costumes were tawdry in the extreme, and their manner of dancing so slow as to seem most monotonous; yet I have never seen more perfect natural grace anywhere displayed than in those measured Spanish dances.

The variety those balls afforded was quite enjoyable until one night a Mexican officer of high rank drew a pistol and fired directly at a man who moved too slowly out of his path to suit the officer's dignity. I never attended another ball, being unwilling to witness such scenes. We had also experienced much difficulty in crossing the Rio Grande at night; so I was glad of an excuse to remain our side of the river after dark, but loved to drive over in broad daylight, when I felt safe and could avoid all midnight perils.

It always seemed to me as if the suave Spanish politeness of those Mexican officers concealed smoldering volcanoes. I have known an officer to shoot a soldier dead at the first hint of insubordination.

We remained at Fort Duncan until early spring, when the mesquite trees, which beautified the parade grounds, were clothed in a tender, fresh green whose tint I have never seen equaled. Our recall to Clark by exchange in March was heartily welcomed.

A cloud, however, loomed on my horizon in the certainty that I must soon leave our dear army life for the East. It is never deemed prudent to remain long in so debilitating a climate, and malarial fever had fastened itself upon both our elder children, completely reducing their strength. We had, however, great cause for thankfulness in their being spared; for the disease was unusually fatal that season, and, indeed, for three long weeks the lives of our little ones hung in the balance, while fear and anxiety harassed our souls.

Texas malarial fever burns with an unremitting ardor nothing can quench until its course has been run. Our good doctor almost lived with us ; and whenever the temperature rose above one hundred and two degrees he would plunge our little boy into a tub of the coldest water procurable, — no ice was to be had, — and hold him there until the child's body became blue, and his teeth began to chatter, when he would be wrapped in blankets, and hot bottles placed at his feet.

Heroic treatment that could not fail to wring a mother's heart! When our little daughter fought the same hard battle for three long weeks, and came out from it a perfect shadow, with her head bald as any infant's, I realized that our physician was right, and that I must leave Texas or we should lose our children.

Better educational facilities also seemed imperative. Thus far I had taught the little ones, and they were well advanced, but no one expects to find very desirable schools in the wilderness ; so we began our preparations for departure, feeling that years must pass before we could again settle down, as education had become the most important need.

CHAPTER XXI.

EXACTLY ten years from the day we had left
New York I returned.   My heart was so bound
up in frontier life I had hoped until the last
moment that the spring rains, which had been
unusually severe, would keep us storm-bound
in Texas.   The town of Brackett had been
flooded just before our departure, and the post,
from its high and dry hill, looked down upon
a scene of devastation and misery.   Every house
on the low lands was undermined, and many
were washed away; the people sought refuge
in trees, where they were obliged to remain for
hours, until assistance in the shape of boats
reached them.

Of course, as in all scenes where the colored
race is conspicuous, several ludicrous incidents
occurred.   One old mammy, who weighed at

least two hundred pounds, in her joy at being rescued, fell into the arms of an unusually small white soldier, and swamped herself, the soldier, and the boat.

Days passed before the water subsided, and in consequence our journey was delayed a month; as with four days of ambulance travel to San Antonio we did not dare start until the roads were dry. I was wicked enough to hope they never would be in condition for travel; but when the mail again reached us regularly there was no farther excuse for delay, and with tearful eyes I bade adieu to dearly loved Fort Clark.

Many of the ladies thought my unwillingness to leave Texas could not be really sincere, a change seemed to them so desirable. But my fears that I should not feel at home in civil life, where everything was so different, were verified.

Four days' travel by ambulance through deep mud was required to reach San Antonio. We did not tarry to explore that curious old town, but stepped immediately on board a train for

Galveston, where we arrived in twenty-four hours. At that place I parted from my husband, and took a steamer for New York. Seven days' passage over Southern and into Northern seas brought us to the city, where our children saw civilization for the first time within their recollections.

It is needless to recount our experiences in New York, or rather Coney Island, where we remained through the summer, and which was just the place for little barbarians to see strange sights and become familiarized with strange scenes.

After all the frontier travel and its dangers through which we had passed, it seemed odd that this land of safety should hardly have been reached before we narrowly escaped serious harm. I chose the boat as a means of transit to Coney Island; and when we reached the pier found that our trunks had not arrived, and so waited hours for the expressman, who did not come until very late in the day.

I was overwhelmed with our belongings,

which consisted of two large trunks, the same number of hand-bags, an immense valise, and a violin. After we had boarded the boat and fairly started on our way, I was dismayed to find night rapidly approaching, and most ominous-looking clouds arising. They proved precursors of a furious storm, the violence of which reminded me of those experienced while at the West. Much damage was done in and around New York Harbor.

When we neared the island after a terrifying trip, I saw to my horror that the boat, instead of landing at the first and completed iron pier, passed it, and made for the uncompleted pier, which jutted much farther out into the ocean, and at that time was simply an uncovered walk about a quarter of a mile in length.

Nothing, however, could be done except land — with three children — and stand in the maddest rush of rain to which I had ever been exposed, watching our trunks and bags tumbled out into the storm. Aware that a few moments' exposure to such a torrent would ruin their contents, I looked, but in vain, for a means of conveyance to the hotel. No one was in sight, the few passengers who had landed having immediately hastened away; and as we were being completely drenched, I decided to leave the baggage to its fate.

Carrying as much as possible in my hands, I sent our little girl in advance with her small brothers. Judge of my horror when suddenly I saw the piles of boards that were stacked in readiness for roofing the pier, moving and actually filling the air on all sides. The children were directly in the path of that furious hurricane, and I could only helplessly watch them. Fortunately it did not last long; and my little daughter was wise enough to race ahead with her brothers, so no damage was done except the loss of both the boys' hats, which blew into the ocean. Then the rain descended with redoubled force; but some one compassionately let us into a little house built for the workmen, where, terrified beyond measure, we were shut in with darkness,

I was all the while worrying about our trunks, and finally induced a workman to promise that he would have them taken to the hotel. But the man soon returned, and reported that they had disappeared. That was a severe blow; and in the darkness I wandered all over the pier until finally a kind policeman was found, who assured me the trunks could not have been stolen. Our search was at last rewarded by their discovery, when the policeman called a coach and bade me take the children to a hotel. I did so, and then sent the coachman back for our trunks.

An hour passed without his return, when I made inquiries, only to be consoled by being told that the coachman was unknown in the hotel, and had probably stolen our possessions.

I started again, in spite of the continued storm, for that pier, where to my joy I spied the policeman, who said he had refused to deliver the trunks without a written order. Although deeply grateful for his caution, I would gladly have been back in Texas, where, whatever happened, there was some one to share hardships with me.

The storm was unusually severe. After its cessation sign-boards were found scattered all over the island, and some buildings had been unroofed.

It is not my intention to dwell at length on our sojourn in the East, which lasted four years. This is a tale of army life, and one accustomed to it is amazed when living among civilians to find how little they know of such an institution as the army.

My husband had long been entitled, by reason of rank and length of service, to the one detail — that of recruiting — which brings a cavalry officer East. He had always intended to reserve this for the time when an education would be demanded for our children, and that time had come; so Mr. Boyd applied for and received the detail in the fall of 1882.

On reaching St. Louis, where the choice of several cities was given him, he selected Boston because of its excellent schools. We spent

there a winter, which seemed to us, fresh from
sunny climes, one long succession of rain, fogs,
and east winds. Still, the many advantages of
that well-regulated city were appreciated, and
had I been well we should have enjoyed its in-
tellectual atmosphere. As it was, we were glad
when summer arrived, and a little cottage on
one of the delightful beaches near by could be
taken. It was a great treat, and we were most
thoroughly enjoying our surroundings, when, in
the month of August, a thunder-clap fell on
our ears in the shape of an order for that Eastern cavalry recruiting station to be discontinued.

Boston had kept the station for so many
years I could not at first believe the bad news
was true. But it proved to be; and Captain
Boyd, who had just received his promotion, was
ordered to open a recruiting office in Davenport, Iowa. After having served faithfully as
lieutenant for twenty-one years, he had at last
been advanced to the rank of captain.

It was not deemed advisable for the entire
family to be continually changing from East to

West, and *vice versâ*, so Captain Boyd went
alone to his new station. Time showed that
our decision had been judicious; for before his
two years of recruiting service were over he
had been assigned to four different stations,
going from Davenport, Iowa, to Rochester, New
York, and finally spending three months at
Jefferson Barracks, Missouri.

Our long planned Eastern tour had proved
an utter failure, and was one more added to the
list of many disappointments. After giving up
our country home near Boston, I went to New
York with our children, and placing them in
excellent schools entered a hospital, where I remained for one long year, a sufferer from illness
entailed by early army hardships. Our little
boy was sent to his grandparents in the country,
and my husband returned to Texas.

After Captain Boyd had been alone there
a year, he asked for and obtained leave of
absence, which permitted us to spend four
pleasant months at Cooperstown, on Otsego
Lake, where we had a glorious time. My hus-

band endeared himself to every one, for he was constantly helping others.

While he was stationed at Davenport, Iowa, a gentleman from there called on me in New York, who described Captain Boyd as the most popular man in the city. He said that every white man, woman, and child in the town knew and loved my husband, while every old darky idolized him.

The ladies connected with one of Davenport's principal churches were greatly in need of money for charitable purposes, and Captain Boyd wrote and delivered a lecture in their behalf which netted nearly three hundred dollars. It was a humorous view of the Indian question, and elicited shouts of applause. He was subsequently invited to give the same address in other cities.

On Captain Boyd's return to the frontier his services as a lecturer were in great demand, and he was in that way able to raise large sums of money for charitable purposes. My husband became the best-known army officer at the West on account of his frequent appearances on the lecture platform.

In the early spring of 1885, four years after having left Texas, I returned. In all that time not one moment had passed in which I would not gladly have been there; so I seized the first plausible excuse afforded — a greatly needed change for our daughter — and leaving the eldest boy at school in New York, again sailed for husband and frontier life.

The sea voyage to Galveston was the most soothing and delightful trip of the kind possible. The water never appears rough immediately after leaving New York; and for three days, while off the coast of Florida, the vessel seemed gently — almost imperceptibly so far as motion was concerned — gliding along. On arriving at San Antonio, instead of a tedious ambulance-ride awaiting us, we went by rail to Fort Clark, which was reached in a few hours.

The sight of dear old familiar landmarks was inexpressibly pleasant; and when we were ushered into one of those well-remembered little houses, with all the old furniture about, it really seemed too good to be true. Everything was more than satisfactory; and the gratification afforded by the change can be understood only by those who have been away from loved scenes for years, and on returning found all expectations realized. Old friends were there to greet us, and we were supremely happy in the renewal of our former life.

My content and joy lasted four months, when rumors of Indian outbreaks in far away New Mexico reached our ears, and were soon followed by an order for all cavalry troops to hold themselves in immediate marching readiness.

Captain Boyd had just returned from a trip to San Antonio, having gone there in compliance with a request to deliver the oration at the National Cemetery on Decoration Day. In that address my husband distinguished himself in a way to be long remembered by his family and friends. It was the most touching and felicitous tribute to our dead soldiers ever written; touching because of the truest sentiments; felicitous because in a place where sectional feeling had for years run riot, not one word was uttered to which the veterans on either side could object.

The address was very lengthy, occupying four columns of the *San Antonio Express,* in which it was published next day; but every word was listened to with eager interest by the immense audience.   Long before its conclusion the fervent tears that fell from old soldiers' eyes attested Captain Boyd's eloquence; and when he ceased speaking the veterans, mainly of the Southern army, crowded about him with words of earnest praise, and begged that he honor them with a visit.   The Texas papers were unanimous in the declaration that no such masterly address had ever before been heard on a similar occasion.

Captain Boyd was obliged to hasten his return because feeling very ill; he had been scarcely able to stand in the heat of that day, May 30, 1885, when, as usual at that season of the year in Texas, the temperature was extreme and the atmosphere torrid.   After reaching home he was confined to his room for a week, and then came word for the troops to start for New Mexico.

The order was received in a telegraphic dispatch from Washington, and was immediately complied with. Before we could realize it, every troop of cavalry had left Fort Clark for an indefinite period. A long series of Apache outrages headed by Geronimo had resulted in the determination to capture him and his band, if it took the whole army to do it. Accordingly, from every post in New Mexico and Texas all troops that could be spared were sent.

A cordon of outposts was established, so that the Indians who had gone into Mexico could not return without being captured. The devastations they had wrought were terrible. The little corner of south-western New Mexico, in the neighborhood of Fort Bayard, had become a veritable charnel house. Every interest of the country had been ruined by their constant raids.

The President's attention was directly drawn to the state of affairs by my brother, who was in Washington at the time. He had edited a paper in Silver City, New Mexico, for several years, and had kept an account of the number of murders committed by Indians — five hundred in eight years. In such a sparsely settled country the loss of so many precious lives was not only sad beyond expression, but if continued must result in hopeless ruin to that region, which, as I have before stated, is the garden spot of the West. Sheltered by numerous hills, cattle always thrive and increase there, because of the perfectly equable climate and a constant supply of nutritive food.

For those very reasons, probably, it was a paradise for the Indians, who could steal in and out more readily on account of the numerous mountain hiding-places.

It was very unusual for troops stationed in Texas to be sent out of their district; but in that case everything possible was done to enhance the safety of the long-suffering people. I shall not try to give an account of that long-protracted warfare, which lasted eighteen months before Geronimo was captured. During that time our troops marched over ground that was well-nigh impassable, and endured every species of hardships. The cavalry worked night and day to secure those wily Indians, and finally succeeded; but a volume would be required if their hardships and sufferings were to be recounted.

It is simply impossible for any one who has not seen the unsettled portions of this country to imagine its character and the difficulties which beset troops that follow on the trails of Indians. Our cavalry has been criticised freely; but I would say to the critic: " Go thou and do likewise." More than they have done, it would be impossible to do, and no country could be less grateful than ours. If soldiers were rewarded according to their deserts, each cavalryman would wear the choicest prize within the nation's gift. The service is very trying. I can scarcely recall an officer who is not a martyr to severe sufferings caused by constant exposure, and who in middle life is not an old man both in feeling and experience.

After reaching Deming, New Mexico, Captain Boyd's troop was sent into the Black Range, where they encamped at a little place called Grafton, fifty miles from the mountains. I have my husband's diary, which contains an account of the march and the country over which they traveled. He greatly disliked to settle quietly down in the camp selected as a permanent one, and was delighted when a letter summoning him away was received.

The letter was sent from a little Mexican town about one hundred miles distant, and informed him that ten Indian women had reached there, who, if captured, would perhaps prove valuable hostages. They were the wives of some members of the band that were on the war-path; and if they could be secured the probability of effecting a treaty seemed reasonable.

Captain Boyd lost no time in preparations, but started at once with twenty mounted men. The march occupied five days, and on reaching the town the Indian women were found in an almost starving condition.

The country was very rough, and a few lines received from my husband while there stated that he was suffering greatly from the effects of bad drinking-water. The man who had sent the letter begged him to remain a few days, and not risk the effects of the return to camp while so ill. But he refused to stay, fearing the Indian women might escape if not speedily taken to a permanent military station.

My husband returned to camp, having suffered intensely during the ten days of his absence, and when he reached his troop was dying, though still refusing to consider himself seriously ill. He at once ordered the only officer with him to proceed with the Indian women to the place where the main body of the regiment was encamped, one hundred and fifty miles distant.

The young officer was so anxious about Captain Boyd that he sent a courier for the nearest surgeon, who was at Hillsboro, eighty miles away. It was four days before the doctor could reach Grafton, and meantime Captain

Boyd was without proper medical attendance. Everything his faithful soldiers could do was done; but, alas, to no purpose! The army doctor's first glance showed him that Captain Boyd was doomed.

For five days the most unremitting care and attention were given him, both by the kind physician and by a captain of the regiment who had accompanied him. But all was useless. The fifth day ended the life of this noble and true man.

Captain Boyd's last hard ride had developed violent inflammation which was simply incurable, as the disease had been increasing for years, having first developed when during the war the young soldier had been compelled to drink impure water and go without food for days. Subsequent years of cavalry hardships had increased its strength until that last exposure proved fatal.

Home in Texas we scarcely realized that he was ill when the terrible news of his death came in a telegram that had been two days *en route*.

Letters had been received from him so regularly that when they ceased I supposed he was still on the march. When the doctor and captain began to write, their communications were at first so encouraging that we could scarcely believe he was in any danger, and were totally unprepared for the terrible sequel. In fact, no one could at first accept the sad truth; for Captain Boyd had been the picture of health, and had impressed every one with his unusual vitality. When the young officer who had been sent forward with the Indian women returned to find his beloved captain dead and buried, the shock was so great he almost fell from his horse.

That Indian campaign resulted in some terrible deaths, but none was more shocking than this sad ending to a long and most faithful career.

Only a few months previously Captain Boyd had spoken very feelingly of the double loss army women sustained when death robbed them of their husbands — the loss of both husband and home. He realized how deeply attached to

the life they became, and how sad it was that
they must be cast adrift from all the associations of years.   But such, though sorrowful in
all its aspects, is the fate of army women.

My grief was intensified by the utter refusal
of the Secretary of War to remove all that
remained of so true and manly a soldier to a
National Cemetery.   After my first request had
been denied I went to Washington, only to
receive there a second from the same source ;
the reason given being that government could
not afford to incur the expense.

Had I not made every effort possible, there
would have been another lonely grave in the
very heart of a remote mountain region, where
none who loved him could ever have visited
the spot.

Captain Boyd died on the same day as General Grant.   A week later orders were received
at Fort Clark from the War Department, direct_
ing that the nation's great general should have
every honor paid his memory.   Guns were
fired, flags displayed at half-mast, and the band

played sad and solemn music, while troops paraded in honor of the dead general and his great achievements.

It seemed to me mournful and unjust, that while high and deserved honors were paid the memory of one, the other, as noble and true a soldier as ever walked this earth, and who had given twenty-four of his forty-one years of life in faithful service, had endured terrible hardships, and yielded at last even his life for his country, should be laid to rest far from home and friends, out on the lonely prairie, and except in the hearts of a few his memory should utterly fade.

Captain Boyd sleeps in the National Cemetery at San Antonio, where six weeks previously he had touched all hearts with his eloquence. Graven on his tomb are the last words of that memorable address :

> " Sleep, soldier, still in honored rest
> Thy truth and valor wearing;
> The bravest are the tenderest,
> The loving are the daring."

APPENDIX A.

Extract from the proceedings of the Association of Graduates of the United States Military Academy at its annual reunion, held at West Point, New York, June 10, 1886.[1]

ORSEMUS B. BOYD.

No. 2216.   Class of 1867.

Died (in the field), at Camp near Grafton, New Mexico, July 23, 1885, aged 41.

"So passed the strong, heroic soul away — "

BORN in New York; appointed from New York; class rank, 61.

Entered the War of the Rebellion as a member of the Eighty-ninth New York Volunteer Infantry, Sept. 1, 1861, and served until July 1, 1863, when he was appointed a Cadet in the United States Military Academy.   He saw active service in our

---

[1] This obituary was distributed throughout the corps of cadets at West Point by the Commandant at the time of Captain Boyd's death, and its perfect justice has never in the slightest degree been challenged.

great war, and was mentioned for gallantry at
Roanoke Island, North Carolina.

He was graduated on June 17, 1867, and appointed second lieutenant Eighth United States
Cavalry; first lieutenant same, Oct. 13, 1868; captain, Jan. 26, 1882.   He died July 23, 1885, closing
in *acknowledged honor* and undoubted manly effec-
tiveness *twenty-four years of faithful and gallant
service* in the saddest of our wars, and in Arizona,
New Mexico, and Texas, where he assisted in developing our great inland resources.

His family have an honest pride in his unosten-
tatious record, and we all may say :

> " Duncan is in his grave.
> After life's fitful fever, he sleeps well."

THE RECORD OF A NOBLE LIFE.

> " I, the despised of fortune, lift mine eyes,
>   Bright with the luster of integrity,
>   In unappealing wretchedness, on high,
>   And the last rage of Destiny defy."

It is with deep solicitude that the writer endeavors, in a few words, to do justice to the memory of
Captain Boyd.

For several long and intensely painful years I
knew him to be an innocent Enoch Arden in a

lonely desert of solitude, bereft of — dearer to the soldier than wife or life — his HONOR — a sufferer for the crime of *another man.*

It was in 1863 that he entered the academy — a veteran soldier, a young man whose merits had gained for him the honorable rank of cadet. In 1864 the writer joined the corps, and for three years marched shoulder to shoulder in the line of the dear old Gray Battalion with the man who sleeps far away from the Hudson, and where the foot of the idle stranger may stop to mark where a good, honest, and much-wronged man sleeps the sleep which knows no waking.

No man ever did better work in the army than Boyd. By steady, faithful, and efficient service, he wore out suspicion, conspiracy, bad luck, and scandal. Since the establishment of his innocence — unsought, unchallenged by him — his defamer has preceded him to the awful bar of the Great Judge.

He lived to round a career of usefulness and gallant service with the tributes of regimental and army respect, the affection of his brother officers, the endearments of family life, the respect of the people of Texas and of the territories where he had served. Demonstrations by his company and comments of the general press prove that his once-shadowed name is now clear and clean, and may be honored by those who loved him.

The facts are these: In the winter of 1865–1866 the robbery of certain sums of money occurred in "B" Company, United States Corps of Cadets. It is unnecessary to refer to the facts other than that after repeated robberies and some rather crude detective work, one evening, at undress parade in the area of barracks, Cadet Boyd was ignominiously brought before the battalion of cadets with a placard of "Thief" on his breast, drummed out of the corps, mobbed and maltreated. A most intense state of excitement prevailed on the post, and the strongest discipline was enforced, the cadets being summarily quelled in any riotous actions. Innocent parties had their names dragged into the affair, and poor Boyd finished his cadetship generally cut in the corps, and endured, till he graduated, a life which was a living hell.

The scandal followed him to his regiment, and years of exemplary behavior were needed to enable him to live down his trouble. His quiet, manly obstinacy in clinging to the army is explained by his innocence. To the honorable but hot-headed men who so long made Boyd carry the burden of another's crime, deepest regret must ever attend the memories of this affair. It is a matter of strange remark that the guilty man who made Boyd suffer for him — John Joseph Casey, of the class of 1868 — was accidentally shot at drill, by a soldier, at Fort Washington, Md., March 24, 1869, within nine months after his apparently honorable graduation. The careers and untimely end of several who bore down on the suffering man of whom we speak show some strange and continued sadness or burdens of expiation. It is all over now. The wandering squadron passing poor Boyd's grave may dip the colors to a man whose eyes closed in honor, true to himself, to his family, his corps and to the dear old flag that he served so patiently, so quietly, and so well. God rest his soul! Amen.

His innocence was publicly established as follows: In the winter of 1867–1868, Cadet Casey, while sick in the hospital, confessed to his roommate, Cadet Hamilton (now dead), that he (Casey) had stolen the moneys for which poor Boyd had suffered the loss of name and fame.

[The records show that Casey was in the hospital from Jan. 24 to Jan. 31, 1868, suffering from dementia. He was so ill that his classmates took turns in nursing him. One night, in his delirium, he spoke of the Boyd affair. Hamilton happened to be with him at the time. The next morning, when Casey was again in a conscious condition, Hamilton told him what he had said. It was *then* that Casey confessed his part of the conspiracy. If it had not been for Casey's illness the facts above narrated would never, in all human probability, have come to light. — *Sec. Assn.*]

It is unnecessary for the writer to state why Hamilton kept this awful secret locked in his breast from 1867–1868 until he died, Jan. 22, 1872, from consumption ; but he did, alas for him ! Casey had peculiar temptations. Private matters and a hounding blackmail pressed him for money, which he stole from rich cadets. The cause was a concealed marriage of Casey's, that if known would have voided his cadetship and destroyed his chance for social elevation.

Poor Boyd lived alone in a room on the third floor, third division, "B" Company. Casey lived directly opposite, and concealed marked money in Boyd's books, which caused Boyd to be suspected as the thief of all the money previously stolen.

Hamilton, the confidant, feared his room-mate of four years, erred, and kept silent, as far as I know, until June, 1871. At the St. Marc Hotel, Washington, D.C., Lieutenant Hamilton, in view of his approaching death, communicated to me his knowledge of Casey's confession and of Boyd's innocence. I was shocked, and at once communicated the facts to the then Lieut. O. B. Boyd, on the frontier. On my return, after three years of absence in the Orient, Europe, and the South, I discovered, in a conversation with Captain Price of the engineers, that full justice had not been done. Duplicate affidavits were immediately made by me and forwarded to Captain Boyd and another person interested. I received a letter from Boyd thanking me for my efforts — a letter that has made me always happy, and which, I regret, is stored with valuable archives where I cannot at once find it. It speaks of his struggles, and pleasantly says that his character needs no present backing, .but that a time will come when I may speak and tell all, if I think it will please those who value him.

It was in Siberia that I received the letter asking me to commit these facts to paper, and by hazard I found a stray copy of the *Army and Navy* which contained a report of Captain Boyd's honorable obsequies.

From the Pacific I pen the last tribute to a man of much-tried worth. The subject brings back painful memories of two men whom I loved and honored in my cadet days — Casey and Hamilton. I am proud to state here that two of my class never cut Boyd, and several others in the corps did him some act of kindness in the awful silence of two years. With pride I recall that the officers of the post did full justice to his barren rights, and that the old and faithful servants of the Academy treated him with a discerning kindness which is a wreath of honor on their silent graves. I will not refer to one affection which cheered him — there are things too sacred for words.

It is all over! There is only one name off the duty roster; an empty chair; a lonely grave; an old sword hanging idly in the sunshine somewhere; a riderless horse; a void in the little family circle which knew and loved the man who is no more.

It is well to know that his name is mentioned with honor and respect; that the burden of another's crime has been cast from him, and that Time will quietly and in honor carpet the grave of the honest soldier with " the grass which springeth under the rain which raineth on the just and the unjust alike." I believe restitution of honor and public consideration has, in so far as possible, been fully made. I look back sadly on my waning youth, as I think of this story, its actors, and that —

" The saint who enjoyed the communion of heaven,
The sinner who dared to remain unforgiven,
The wise and the foolish, the guilty and just,
Have quietly mingled their bones with the dust."

RICHARD H. SAVAGE,
Class of 1868.

APPENDIX B.

AMERICAN CIVILIZATION.

AS VIEWED BY WEEPING WEASEL, LATE CHIEF OF THE KIOWAS.

A LECTURE

Written by CAPTAIN· ORSEMUS BRONSON BOYD, *in behalf of the Charitable Enterprises of the Ladies connected with the —— Church of Davenport, Iowa, and also given before the Masonic Lodge in San Antonio, Texas.*

Ladies and Gentlemen : — In the first place I am not a lecturer. I make this announcement now, for fear you may not discover it before I shall have finished, or if the fact should be rudely thrust upon you, I will have pleaded guilty in advance to the indictment.

When, a boy, I took part in the debating clubs that were held in those old red schoolhouses where all great affairs of state — wars, revolution, politics and finance — were discussed with the freedom of boys and the ignorance of savages, there was one question which never failed to elicit ample talk: " Resolved, that anticipation is better than reality," and on that question I was always in the affirmative. In an hour you will all be with me.

I shall tell no tale of personal adventure; nothing worth recording ever happened to me. Diogenes, with a lantern, and open sunlight to aid the lantern, in the city of Athens failed to find an honest man. An untutored Indian from the plains of Texas, amid the common events and every day life of the Pale-faces, discovered that their vaunted civilization was a myth, and their boasted culture a delusion. Let us at once annihilate the Indian and discredit Diogenes.

In common with all Christians of our kind, we believe that it is easier for a camel to go through the eye of a needle than for a rich man to inherit the kingdom of heaven. There are other Christians who believe that it is easier for a rich man to go through the eye of a needle than for a camel to inherit the kingdom of heaven. Who shall say which Christian is *the* Christian ?

Before the brothers of this noble profession, this mystic tie, whose deeds have been known in every

land and under every sun — amid burning flames
and on frozen mountains, on swollen rivers and
tempestuous seas, by the bedsides of dying princes,
in the cabins of poverty, desolation, and disease,
in public and private, to bond and free, to all
brothers who own its symbolic rites — to all
brothers and wives of the brothers, I can more
freely speak of one who, though ignorant and a
savage, still found in his own faith and his own
civilization his own Christianity.

Eighteen hundred years ago, in Capernaum by
the Sea of Galilee, a man, whom the charity of
God had sent into the world, was preaching to the
people. And a certain lawyer, willing to justify
himself, stood up and asked, " Who is my neighbor ? " Promptly came the answer:

" A certain man went down from Jerusalem to
Jericho, and fell among thieves, which stripped
him of his raiment, and wounded him, and departed, leaving him half dead.

" And by chance there came down a certain
priest that way, and when he saw him he passed
by on the other side.

" And likewise a Levite, when he was at the
place, came and looked on him, and passed by on
the other side.

"But a certain Samaritan as he journeyed, came where he was; and when he saw him, he had compassion on him.

"And went to him, and bound up his wounds, pouring in oil and wine, and set him on his own beast, and brought him to an inn, and took care of him.

"And on the morrow when he departed, he took out two pence, and gave them to the host, and said unto him, Take care of him: and whatsoever thou spendest more, when I come again, I will repay thee.

"Which now of these three, thinkest thou, was neighbor unto him that fell among the thieves?"

On the boundless prairies of the West and South, that are in extent empires, the white man has learned that devotion which Nature, in her grandest forms, most surely teaches. He has learned that tolerance which men unfettered by the bonds of conventional society most quickly learn.

Two years ago last July I found myself encamped upon the banks of the Red River of Texas, with forty horsemen as scouts under my command. Like a silver thread the river ran a thousand feet beneath us, through the wildest and most precipitous cañon.

At four o'clock one morning, a Seminole Indian, attached to the command, brought me intelligence that six hours previously six horses, four lodges, one sick Indian, five squaws, and several children had descended into the cañon one mile above us, and were then lost to sight.   I asked:

" Had they provisions ? "

" Yes ; corn and buffalo meat."

" How do you know ? "

" Because I saw corn scattered upon one side of the trail, and flies had gathered upon a piece of buffalo meat on the other."

" How do you know that one of the Indians is sick ? "

" Because the lodge poles were formed into a travois, that was drawn by a horse blind in one eye."

" How do you know the horse was half blind ? "

" Because, while all the other horses grazed upon both sides of the trail, this one ate only the grass that grew upon one side."

" How do you know the sick one was a man ? "

" Because when a halt was made all the women gathered around him."

" Of what tribe are they ? "

" Of the Kiowa tribe."

And thus, with no ray of intelligence upon his stolid face, the Seminole Indian stood before me and told all I wished to know concerning our new neighbors, whom he had never seen.

Two hours from that time, not knowing whether they were friends or enemies, I was carefully studying, from the bluff above, through a field-glass, the Indian camp.

The lodges had all been erected, and were gay with the robes of the buffalo of the plains, the prairie wolf, and the coyote. A great war bonnet of eagles' feathers hung before the door of the principal tepee, denoting that its occupant was a chief. From the lodge pole floated a blue streamer, bearing the rude device, in red paint, of a whip-poor-will attacking a rattlesnake; this told me that he was the chief of all the Kiowas. I knew the man. I had met him, with many others of his tribe, one night several years before, one hundred miles below on the same river, and the meeting had not been pleasant to either of us.

In fact, several hours had been required in which to adjust our differences ; and as the chief left me amid the crack of rifles and the swish of arrows, I heard his clear voice solemnly declaring in Span-ish that he would surely come again " when the

moon was young." Fate was too strong even for
the chief of the Kiowas; he never came; his tribe
had been conquered and were at peace.

Returning to my cantonment, I hastily saddled
a small detachment, and descending the almost
precipitous sides of the gorge reached the Indian
encampment, and dismounting, raised the buffalo
skin that hung before the entrance of the principal
lodge, and stood unsummoned in the presence of
the chief. An old and shriveled man, with nerveless arms and sunken eyes, from which the fire of
battle had forever fled, lay upon a rude couch of
skins. He gave courteous greeting, said he knew
me, and even spoke my name. As I sat upon the
ground at his side he told me how, for weeks
before our previous meeting to which I have
alluded, he had been upon my trail when I marched
over the short, crisp buffalo grass of the staked-
plains. He had known my personal habits, the
disposition of the camp for defense at night, the
number of men, animals, and wagons; in fact, all
that I had known myself.

The chief then told me that he was stricken by
death, and should soon be in the presence of the
Great Spirit, roaming the happy hunting grounds
of his tribe, and asked that he be allowed to die
in peace.

Day after day I visited the dying warrior, who related from time to time, as his strength permitted, the story of his life and the story of his tribe. He recounted the wrongs they had suffered, and the wrongs they had done. He told me of their customs and traditions, their marriages, births, and deaths. For days he talked, sometimes in the soft Spanish tongue, often in the beautiful sign language of the plain Indian.

In my youth I lived near, and of course read the romantic creations of that clever gentleman who resided upon the shores of the beautiful Cooperstown Lake. I had also read the works of a novelist from the South who had invested the Indian character with all the warmth and color of his native skies, with all the romance that belonged to his Southern forests, gay with flowers and poetic with festoons of clinging moss.

In consequence of this I had come to look upon the Indian as all that was noble, grand, and heroic in war, all that was gentle, tender, and true in peace. I had read with breathless interest of his loves, courtships, and marriages. I had admired his keenness of vision upon the trail, his untiring energy, fleetness of foot, immunity from fatigue, his long fasts, and the halo of romance that seemed to ever encircle him. I considered him a " Chevalier Bayard," a model of physical beauty, who resembled, perhaps, the dying gladiator.

My boyhood's dream was rudely broken, and like many another boyish illusion it disappeared in a day. I found the Indian dirty, unwashed, and treacherous, a prey to the lowest instincts and the most revolting cruelty.

He was no " Chevalier Bayard," and did not resemble the dying gladiator. The romance, color, light and shades — all were gone, and I learned that the Indian and our treatment of him were deformities and blots upon our fair land and our modern civilization. Between the law of force upon one side, and the law of civilization upon the other, the Indian has been tossed like an unripe apple, and has not known which to obey.

One night the old Indian chief died, and the next morning, with such rude and simple rites as obtained among the Kiowas, we carried him to his last resting place upon the platform which had been erected for the purpose.

The dawning light was flushing rosy red in the blushing East; in the West the darkness of the night still lingered. The songs of a thousand birds and the chirp of millions of insects broke in some measure the eternal silence of those great plains. The buzzard, a mere speck in the sky, with the eye of the eagle waited impatiently for his prey. Herds of timid antelopes, with great startled eyes, watched us from a distance, ready to dash away on fleetest foot at a moment's warning. Troops of buffaloes were slaking their thirst in the rippling river. The great cat-fish, with strong leaps, rose bodily from the water in pursuit of prey, and fell back with a splash.

All animal life was awake with the flush of the morning; and as the sun's disk appeared above the horizon's dead level, we laid the chief upon the platform, with his face turned toward the " God of the Dome." His body was wrapped in a red blanket stoutly bound about with cords. He had been brave in battle, so all his war implements were laid by his side. His great war bonnet of eagle's feathers was hung upon one of the upright poles. His horses were slain by the scaffold. Then, to the accompaniment of low-voiced chants, his widows began their work of scarification with knives upon the lower extremities. When that was finished we left him to the hush of those vast plains.

That night in one of the lodges a great great

granddaughter but a few months old died. The child was placed in a frail burial canoe, covered with trailing vines that had grown upon the river's banks, and gently cast adrift. No doubt the tiny bark was soon caught in rippling eddies, or its course stopped by stout rushes, and in time its lifeless occupant returned to the dust from which it had sprung.

After the obsequies of the dead chief I returned to camp, and in order to divert my mind sought to fatigue my body by stalking buffaloes all day. But I had gained a new insight into the Indian character, and one which enabled me to respect it.

That evening, lying in a hammock under the awning of my tent, as the first shades of darkness came creeping over the plains, there struck upon my ears, borne upward from the gorge below, the chant of Indian women for their dead. Its tones were the rhythm of sorrow and the notes of woe. Until midnight the songs continued, now loud, then sinking to the faint whisperings of the wind. Next morning the lodges were in ashes, and nothing was left of our strange neighbors but the dead chief upon his platform, and the footprints of their moccasins as they traveled straight toward the North Star.

These events made so strange and strong an impression upon me, that I propose telling you this evening, in as simple words as possible, the story of the pilgrimage of Weeping Weasel, late chief of all the Kiowas. I shall dwell longer upon his attempts to introduce the white man's civilization in his tribe, what he saw, and the inferences drawn therefrom, than upon all the other incidents he related. The conclusions at which Weeping Weasel, with the intellect of an Indian and the sagacity of a politician, arrived, are not necessarily mine; and if their recital should wound any one within the sound of my voice, I would beg them to remember that they were told me by a dying Indian chief, as he lay in his lodge upon the banks of the Red River flowing peacefully through the great staked-plains of Texas.

Years and years before — even for hundreds of summers — the Kiowas had been a powerful nation. When the tent of the chief was planted, there clustered around it five thousand lodges. The tribe was rich in the implements of war, owned thousands of horses, were mighty hunters, bold and aggressive warriors. No footprint of man or animal, no upturned stone, broken twig or bended grass escaped the keen vision of their scouts.

From El Paso, where the Rio Grande del Norte commences its westward course, and swings in the arc of a great circle until completed at the mouth of the Pecos, where it again flows south, they owned the lands of which this river formed the Western boundary ; thence south across the "Devil's River" and the Nueces, to where it empties into beautiful Matagorda Bay. On the east they had fought for supremacy with the Comanches, and been victorious. They had made the Tonkawas a nation of beggars and old women. From across the border they had repelled invasions of the Kickapoos and Lipan-Apaches. They had marched, an irresistible army, across the pine ridges and cedar mountains of New Mexico, and fearlessly confronted the Warm Springs and Mescalero tribes. The Utes of Colorado had descended from their mountain fastnesses, battled with them in the open plain, and been defeated. They had measured lances with and beaten the Tonto and Jicarrila — Apaches of Arizona. They had destroyed the great wheat-fields on the Gila River of the Pima and Maricopa tribes. The Yumas had heard their battle-cry. They had pushed their conquests amongst the Pi-Utes and Shoshones of Nevada, and from thence had marched against the

Bannocks of Idaho, and the Nez Perces of Oregon. Their spoils of war had been great.

But in course of time the hands of all other tribes were raised against them, and through disaster and defeat they had been reduced to the occupancy of only the great plains of Western Texas.

At that time Weeping Weasel became their chief. He was then in the prime of manhood. The nerveless arm that I saw in his lodge could then draw the six-foot arrow to its head, and make the cord of deer sinews writhe and moan as in pain.

He saw that peace and industry would perhaps be of great benefit to his tribe, and after much communion with himself and consultation with the elders, concluded at no distant day to turn his face toward the rising sun, and learn the strange and barbarous ways of the Pale-faces. He had been told they were as numberless as the leaves of the forest when the hot sirocco that comes from the southern islands shakes them with its fiery breath.

Marching over these great and silent plains under the blazing sun, he had learned in some instinctive way that the Pale-faces would build cities there, and people them with busy men and women.

Weeping Weasel had seen the *Pongo* or smoke-man in the North that traversed its iron rails faster than his fleetest pony could gallop. He had seen a small wire stretched on poles through which he could but dimly comprehend that the men who lived at the rising sun talked with their brothers who lived at the setting sun.

But before starting on a journey so fraught with peril, he thought best to call to his aid teachers — those of good repute among the Pale-faces. Through a missionary he secured the ser-vices of two devotees from Massachusetts, who came and opened a school for the boys and girls of his tribe.

It is true that in visage and mien these teachers did not resemble the dusky beauties of the Kiowa race. The ringlets worn at the side of the face, the eyes that looked through strange pieces of glass, the mysterious scrolls which they held in their hands, and the sounding fall of a heavy foot instead of the dewy touch of the moccasin, were not calculated to inspire love and respect from un-tutored savages.

Still, with the devotion of their calling, and in

their desire to do good, these mistaken and mis-guided women taught on. But one fatal day they were surprised by Weeping Weasel while teaching the children that the world is round. The Kiowas believed it to be flat. Weeping Weasel, with the decision worthy a general of iron nerve and un-flinching courage in the right, seized and burned them at the stake.

He scattered their ashes to the four winds of heaven, and in a long address to the Historical Society of Boston, asked that others with less pernicious doctrines be sent. It is perhaps need-less to state that even the old Bay State, with its advanced ideas and unyielding principles, could find no more volunteer missionaries for that work. Therefore Weeping Weasel must needs start upon his pilgrimage toward the rising sun.

The night previous to his departure all the tribes assembled, and with the great Southern Cross gleaming and burning, they performed the sacred rites and mysteries of the sun dance. A hundred fires flamed brightly. Amid the yells of warriors and the shrieks of those fainting from self-inflicted tortures, there arose the monotonous chants of the women as they prayed for the safety of their chief.

At break of day he left them, and a great silence fell upon the tribe as they mournfully sought their separate lodges.

Day by day Weeping Weasel traveled north and east, sleeping at night under the stars, his food procured by bow and arrow, his drink taken from limpid streams.

At last he came to the country of the "Smoke-man," and taking passage was borne swiftly over mountains and through the valleys to some bluffs upon the boundary of a great State, where other Indians had held their councils years before, and where he determined to commence his researches and investigations.

His pilgrimage becoming known, the chief was hospitably lodged in the house of a Christian gentleman of that town who was a land agent. Among the Kiowas the title to all lands and the occupancy thereof were considered sacred. Even in their forays against other tribes they contended for supremacy, not for a title to the country. Indeed, so strong was this honesty implanted in the breast of the savage and barbarous Indian, that once, after a great battle with the Comanches, rather than do violence to this principle he had ceded to them a thousand square miles of his own country, deeming that better than to question such undoubted right.

The land agent showed him, in his office, maps of lands which bore strong resemblance to those occupied by his tribe. Upon leaving, this same Christian gentleman followed him across the State to a city with a great bridge and offered to sell, beseeching him to buy, for a merely nominal sum, thousands and thousands of acres upon which his tribe had dwelt from time immemorial. Weeping Weasel determined not to incorporate the land usages of the Pale-faces amongst his people.

In the towns and camps of the Kiowas, great attention had been paid to the sanitary conditions of their immediate surroundings. This was necessary for the life and health of individual members of the tribe.

In that city by the bridge he found the people in a certain locality stricken unto death by a strange pestilence. Upon investigating the cause, he learned they all had drank water from a certain well. Weeping Weasel concluded that, if he were the chief in this locality, there would be sewers and water-mains; or failing these, the inhabitants who refused or were too indolent to carry water from the river would receive a punishment, compared with which the cholera would be a lingering and painless death. But Weeping Weasel was an untaught, rude, and barbarous savage.

The "Father of Waters" next attracted the attention of this curious pilgrim. Compared with all other rivers he had ever seen, it was as the sun to the faintest twinkling star. He worshiped it as a god. Day by day he sat upon the banks, watched it through all changing moods, loved it best when angry currents brought down yellow mud from the far North, and worshiped it most when the setting sun's ocher light fell upon its surging waters, enveloping beautiful islands.

There floated upon its broad expanse numberless strange monsters, propelled in some mysterious way. Weeping Weasel found they carried grain, fruit, and other produce from one part of the country to another, and then first began to understand the law of trade — of barter and sale. He took passage upon one of these palaces, descending a hundred miles; saw the busy towns upon the banks of his idol, filled, as he thought, with crazy men and women. Why all this rush, ceaseless activity and strife for wealth, he questioned.

Returning at night, and standing upon the deck with head uncovered in the reverent attitude a

savage always assumes when awe-stricken in the
presence of nature, he suddenly became conscious
of a strange throbbing through every fiber of the
monster.   He also saw abreast another monster all
aglow with fire; men were shouting and running
like mad!   Every few minutes its huge furnace
doors were opened, and the blazing fires fed with
pitch and resin.   The vessel shook in every joint;
men and women were crowding the deck all hoarse
from shouting; money was freely changing hands;
from the smoke-stacks long lines of fire trailed out
through the darkness ; the gurgling water at the
bow was thrown in spray upon the deck.   Suddenly
there was a terrible roar, a great flash of fire, then
darkness came, and Weeping Weasel knew no more
until he found himself safe upon the river's bank.

He was told that a hundred men, women, and
children had been sacrificed that night.   Burning
with anger and righteous indignation, Weeping
Weasel attended the coroner's inquest; the evidence was conflicting; no one in particular seemed
to have been to blame; it was an accident.   Weeping Weasel went forward to offer his testimony ; a
savage could not take the oath.   The coroner's
jury promptly acquitted all of blame, even the
poor Indian, and the event was soon forgotten.

Weeping Weasel determined that the civilization of the steamboat should never be introduced among his people.

Again he turned his face to the east, and traveled across a great State where the fields were waving with ripening grain. Neat farmhouses had been erected on every side. The corn and wheat that he saw growing seemed to him of no use. Who would require it?

On these undulating plains with cattle, sheep, and horses, where peace and plenty seemed to reign and the merry voices of children were heard at sunset, our untutored savage began to think perhaps was the civilization of which he had dreamed. Still he had the Indian's caution, and arrived at conclusions slowly.

He determined to abide three days in the most peaceful and quiet village, and chose one with two churches, a bank, and store.

Upon awakening the first morning, he found that the store had been robbed and burned during the night. The following day the two churches were in fierce dispute over some minor point of doctrine. The third morning it was learned that the bank cashier had absconded with all the funds, leaving hundreds of families destitute.

The Kiowas did not steal from each other; the simple faith in the Great Spirit which they had in common furnished no cause for dispute; and the custodian of the tribe's public goods never ran away with them. They never had thought of such an occurrence; and the event was so improbable that those barbarous savages had not even prescribed a mode of punishment for it.

Weary, harassed, tormented, and worn-out even at the commencement of his pilgrimage, Weeping Weasel would gladly have turned his face toward the setting sun; but patience being one of the great virtues of the Kiowas, he again girded up his loins and proceeded on his journey.

But a great fear was coming upon his superstitious soul. One afternoon, years before, while hunting, Weeping Weasel had fallen asleep by the side of a spring that bubbled from beneath an immense boulder, which was sufficiently large to protect him from the sun's rays. As he slept, there appeared before him the god Stone-Shirt, followed by Pantasco, or he who robs the living; Kay-Wit, he who robs the dead; and Quite-Qui, who robs both living and dead. All passed before the sleeping warrior, to whom Stone-Shirt foretold in the sign language this pilgrimage and the events which would follow.

Weeping Weasel could only dimly comprehend on awaking, that in case of failure he was to be turned into one of the three horrid shapes shown him by Stone-Shirt; and, forever shut out from the Great Spirit and the happy hunting grounds, his soul, without arms to defend itself, must wander and fall through unfathomable space and darkness.

When he saw the terrible anxiety, woe, and despair written upon the faces of fathers, mothers, and children whom the vandal acts of the faithless cashier had ruined, Weeping Weasel concluded to ever pray that he be not turned into the horrid shape which steals from the living.

In the robbery of the store the proprietor had been killed; and as this ignorant savage gazed upon the form of the man who had died while defending his property, Weeping Weasel, in the agony of his soul, prayed to Stone-Shirt that he be spared, both in this his mortal, and in his future spiritual, existence, assuming the form of him who robs the dead.

In the dispute between the churches, so much rancor and venom had been developed that men who were peacefully lying, as they had lain for years, in the little cemetery of the town, were publicly discussed, and motives and opinions the worst imputed to them. Happily they were ignorant of all this.

The living were slandered and the dead vilified. Brother became the enemy of brother, sisters were estranged, husbands and wives separated. Again Weeping Weasel besought Stone-Shirt, and with the sweat of mortal agony upon his brow, that, if he must, he would face either of the two horrible shapes to be spared the form of the one who robs both the living and the dead.

Weeping Weasel soon found himself in a great city by a lake. Here he was lodged in the house of a gray-haired and respectable man, a pillar of the church, and one who gave largely, in an indiscriminate way, to churches and the poor. He had no time to investigate charities, and only contributed to them because he had money, or perhaps to ease the gnawings of a conscience not altogether dormant.

Weeping Weasel was taken to church, where an eloquent preacher held his audience spell-bound as he impressed upon it the evils of gambling. To all his strictures the gray-haired man responded with fervent "Ahmens!"

The next morning his host escorted Weeping

Weasel to a great mart of trade in that populous city. There the savage Indian remembered the immense wheat and corn fields he had passed as he journeyed east. He saw the reverend gentleman who had spoken so eloquently on the sin of gambling stealthily enter a broker's office and sell thousands and thousands of bushels of grain which he did not own, and never would. His gray-haired entertainer, who had so graciously responded " Ahmen ! " stood in the center of hundreds of other men, all of whom were shouting and howling as he drove grain up and down by a nod of his head ; men were ruined and families made destitute by this man, who called gambling a sin.

Weeping Weasel learned, but it was difficult to grasp the idea, that crops were bought and sold before they were sown ; that they became a football upon " Change," even while growing ; and when finally sent to market they ruined thousands. He found that all this disastrously affected the poor brethren of the Pale-faces, and that children were hungry in consequence. The chief decided he would grow only enough corn to satisfy the wants of his people, and would forever remain silent in regard to the gambling transactions.

Once in the history of the Kiowa tribe an old

and respected warrior had been selected to build a lodge in which public meetings were to be held. He was to be paid from the goods owned in common. To the dismay and horror of all, it was found that this rude architect had not been honest; he had demanded more buffalo hides than were needed for the building, and the best he had conveyed to his own lodge, and afterward sold to wandering traders. When the man's crime became known he was seized, and the elders sat around him with stern visages. His trial was short; he was bound on the top of the dishonestly built lodge, and met his death in its flames.

Weeping Weasel was shown a great hall of justice in that city where the granite was the finest and the workmanship the most skillful. He was told that the builder had taken the best granite and sold it to the traders among the Pale-faces. Thinking this had just been discovered, our barbarous Indian went early the next morning to witness the destruction of the building and cremation of the dishonest builder. He waited until noon, and as the building still stood and no torch had been applied, Weeping Weasel turned sorrowfully away just in time to see the false builder drinking champagne at a fashionable restaurant with his friends. This phase of civilization would not do for the fierce and warlike Kiowas.

The right of husbands to exact obedience, and the duty of wives to obey, was one of the laws of the Kiowas, as unalterable as if written upon tablets of stone. So strongly was this doctrine implanted in the breast of the savage that once, in a foray against a Northern tribe, a favorite squaw of Weeping Weasel's had, in direct disobedience to his command, followed a distance of two days' march and entered his lodge at nightfall. She was beautiful then; but when I saw her on the banks of the Red River she was disfigured. A broken collar bone and a flattened nose were the results of her disobedience. She returned quickly; her only cause of anxiety being that she could not travel nights for fear of passing her own village.

But among the Pale-faces Weeping Weasel learned that the custom was different. He found the wife frittered away her time while the husband was at the counting-room or office. If he commanded her to abstain from the round dances, she danced them; if he ordered her east, she went west; if he asked her to attend church, she preferred the opera; if he expressed a desire for the sea-shore, she chose the mountains of New Hampshire. Weeping Weasel, with the cunning of the savage, decided that this should never be told the squaws of his nation.

As no man, intent upon a great mission, can hope to escape annoyances and observation from the idle, vulgar, and indolent, this warrior from the South found that his wearing apparel, the dress of his fathers, and the habit of his tribe, was a matter of curious comment even among those busy people. His clothes were good enough for him, and there were no fashion plates and paper patterns in use among the Kiowas. Still, at a council held at one time for the general good of the tribe, a daring innovator had, as a protection against snakes while marching, suggested that the boots of the Pale-face be adopted. A pair had been found amongst their war plunder at one time, and had been examined curiously by all the tribe.

In an institution for the sick, Weeping Weasel saw in a padded cell a maniac, confined and chained to the floor. He held a wisp of straw in his mouth, his clothes were torn to tatters, his hands cut and bleeding, foam issued from his mouth and mingled with blasphemy from his lips. His cries for salvation from invisible enemies were piteous. The matted hair and bloodshot eye told the Indian a tale as graphic as the pictured rocks of his own tribe. He found that the man was young, rich, and respected. He asked the nature of the disease, and was carelessly told that it was "snakes in his boots." Sadly Weeping Weasel asked that the wire be at once ordered to carry a message to his tribe for the immediate destruction of the boots found among their plunder. He also wondered why the Pale-faces did not at once destroy the serpent whose terrible folds were coiling around the youth of their country.

All this time Weeping Weasel's perceptions were being quickened and his reasoning powers enlarged. The Kiowas had always considered the marriage tie sacred. It was true a man might have many wives, enough to do all the work of his lodge, while he used his energies only for war or in the pursuit of game. But once taken, the man and woman were bound for life. No power on earth could dissolve the tie. Infidelity in either was punished by death. But in that great city he found courts open as the day, in which shameless men and brazen women sought the strong arm of the law to break and tear asunder the most sacred and binding of oaths. Weeping Weasel learned that only a publication in an obscure newspaper was necessary to satisfy the goddess whom Weeping Weasel had seen represented as blind-folded, with scales in her hand. Incompatibility of temperament was often the cause alleged. This the Indian could not understand. Among the Kiowa husbands and wives such a thing was unknown. The husband commanded, the wife obeyed. Weeping Weasel found after a time that this term was used to indicate that wives had become tired of their husbands, or husbands had grown weary of their wives. It often meant dishonest and unholy loves, and could be construed as indicative of a thousand things when the cord that first bound two people together had become a gnawing, corroding chain of iron.

The ignorant savage had not as yet found any advantage to be gained from the civilization of the Pale-faces. Weary and sick at heart, the pilgrim pushed on until he reached the chief city of the great nation. He had begun to comprehend the numbers of the Pale-faces and their strength. His brain was confused. He was so torn by conflicting emotions that he feared his judgment would become warped and valueless. Arriving in the great city, he learned that a man with unlimited power had betrayed his trust and plundered the city's treasury of millions. Yet the blind goddess had thrown around him all possible shields to cover his glaring rascality. He had banded with him an army of thieves. Again a great hall of justice had been the means used to rob and plunder the people at will. Before public exposure the thing had been a byword and a jest at the clubs.

The man who had done all this had risen to power from the ranks of the common people. Weeping Weasel wondered if he had risen to power by his rascality. But conscious that he was ignorant and a savage, he rejected the thought as unmanly.

When a warrior among the Kiowas betrayed a public trust he was terribly punished. But one such case had ever been handed down in the traditions of their tribe. In that instance the culprit had been led in a circle surrounded by all his tribe — every man, woman, and child was present — the silence was fearful; then the body of the victim was covered with the broad leaves of the prickly pear, and they were one by one set on fire. The punishment seemed to have been effectual.

Next morning our Indian appeared at the city hall to witness the torture; again he waited until noon, and as no steps had been taken against the wrong-doer, he concluded, to say the least, that the white man was slow in punishing criminals.

The Kiowas had always paid great attention to the rearing of their children, and especially exercised great care and foresight over the girls, who were to become future mothers of the warriors of the tribe. No Indian girl of six or twelve years could be absent from her lodge after the fall of evening dew. She knew no lovers until she had arrived at the age and estate of womanhood. Among the Pale-faces this custom did not obtain. Weeping Weasel saw misses of tender age, in pinafores, give large parties to other children; boys were invited. He saw childish eyes sparkle with bandied jest and compliments fit only for mature years. He saw children, excited by the dance, intoxicated with music, satiated with rich food, spend the best hours of the night in gay and reckless dissipation.

At certain seasons of the year the Chickasaw plum furnished much of the food used by his tribe. If the pure white dust was brushed from its surface when half-ripe, it never fruited in perfection. Weeping Weasel found that the Pale-faces often brushed the dust of the plum from the cheek of childhood.

The Kiowa woman was to him the model of physical beauty; her large waist, broad, strong shoulders, the strength of limb, elastic, springing step, and downcast eyes were such as he deemed fitting for women who were to rear the future braves of their race.

Among the Pale-faces he found that maternity was a burden to be avoided; that the waist was contracted by springs of steel; the body thrown forward at an angle upon the hips by strong pieces of wood placed under the heels; the face was covered by a vile compound which looked like flour, or was painted as the savage paints when he marches to battle or prepares for the sun dance. Curious to ascertain the exact value of all this nonsense he made calculation, and learned that the muslin and silk, velvet and ribbons, paint and powder, flowers and bits of steel, amounted to about four hundred and fifty-three dollars. That is to say, in the Kiowa computation, forty-five and a half horses.

Weeping Weasel determined to be silent upon this manifest absurdity of the Pale-face women.

The Kiowa women wore the hair straight down their backs and combed away from their eyes. The daughters of the Pale-faces cut theirs short in front and allowed it, except when curled by hot irons, which the damp strangely affected, to fall into their eyes. The meaning and mystery of this Weeping Weasel never attempted to fathom.

Besides the Great Spirit whom the Kiowas worshiped in common, each Indian had a personal god to whom alone he was responsible. This god was the conscience of the savage, and above it was only the commands of the Great Spirit. His religion was always with him; it was his shield and strength in the day of battle, his comfort in time of peace : he heard it in the whispering of the wind and the sighing of the trees ; he recognized it in the rustle of the growing grass and the ripening grain; he felt it in the songs of birds and the whirr of insects' wings. It warned him in the broken watch-spring buzz of the deadly rattlesnake ; in the forms of the clouds he saw it; in the flush of morning and the darkness of evening he knew it. It was his only ideal of the estate of future happiness where game would be plenty and peace eternal. The bark on which these mysteries were written was to him sacred. The savage accepted as truth its teachings, which long generations of Kiowas had confirmed.

He went while in that city to hear a speaker —

silver-tongued and magnetic, who had all the graces which belong to the polished orator; his voice was like the sound of bells to the Indian, whose nature is ever open to the charm of this God-like gift. But he heard the man revile, distort, and falsify the religion of the white man. He heard him read from the sacred book, with laughing mien and careless jest, most solemn promises. The mysteries of the creation and the origin of the Pale-faces became in the mouth of this man as intangible as the will-o'-the-wisp he had seen floating over his Southern swamps.

Listening to him, and applauding to the echo, were sons and daughters of the Pale-faces. Fair women and intelligent men accepted as eternal truth the words of the speaker. Weeping Weasel was ashamed, astonished, dismayed! In this desecration of religion the wild Indian of the Southern plains thought he could dimly comprehend the future downfall of a great nation.

The pilgrim lost hope. Still he determined to pursue the subject to its bitter end, and went one bright morning to the City of Churches. Business had ceased, and the streets were quiet. In a darkened temple, rich with stained glass, the air heavy with burning incense, and stirred only by the notes of a great organ as it kept time to the voices of boys who sang in angelic tones the litany of the church, he heard an eloquent preacher tell of the wickedness and sin of two great cities; and how, because not ten righteous men could be found therein, they were destroyed from the face of the earth. He also listened to the story of the wife who looked back, and was turned into a pillar of salt. The next morning Weeping Weasel bought a canopy of asbestos roofing, and thereafter never appeared in the streets of either of the cities without carrying it above his head.

Again he was shown the great marts of trade, larger than the grain exchange of another city. Here men bought and sold scraps of paper and the country's gold. It was the same old scenes. Stocks went up and down by a nod of the head, and again men were made poor in a moment. The ruined ones were driven from the exchange, and forever after, with wild eyes and fevered pulse, they haunted its doors and talked, with the strange infatuation of the Indian hemp-eater, of the rise and fall of the stocks that had ruined them.

One terrible day Weeping Weasel saw a coin that the Pale-face used in exchange for goods become enhanced in value three times. Wild, haggard men clung to railings for support, so faint they could not stand. Two unprincipled members of the exchange were the agents of this scheme. When night came, the credit of the country had been nearly ruined. The two conspirators slunk to a hotel that was soon surrounded by a howling mob. Trade and industry were impaired, commerce nearly swept from the sea and land, and credit almost lost by the act of those two men. Weeping Weasel again determined that gambling should forever be prohibited among his people, even the throw of the six cherry stones for a quart of Chickasaw plums.

Among the Kiowas the public singer of the tribe's heroic deeds was a warrior, always well paid for his services. He had the warmest seat in the lodge, and at the feast of dog-meat the tenderest piece; but the newspaper man of the Palefaces was lean, ill-fed, and most lightly paid. Weeping Weasel found that medicines for the cure of all diseases were sold in bottles, and that the proprietors waxed rich. The savage concluded that all the Pale-faces could drink, but that few could read.

In settling disputes among the Kiowas, all matters in question were referred to a council composed of fifteen elders of the tribe. Each principal laid his case before the tribunal with all the clearness possible, in order that a just decision might be reached. Among the Pale-faces the Indian found a class of men skilled in the preparation of causes in dispute. From long practice, close study, and great care, these men, who talked only of others' rights and not of their own, had become so skillful that white was made black, and black white, as each argued his own point. Doubt was thrown upon the most open and public transactions. Witnesses swore to the most improbable events, and to occurrences they had never seen. In their harangues before the elders each quoted the same statutes in the same words, as applicable to his side of the cause. There were fierce disputes and incessant wrangling. Weeping Weasel determined that this kind of practice should never obtain a footing in his tribe.

The Kiowas had always considered sacred the life of each member of the tribe. In their rude and barbarous code there was no deviation from the rule of " blood for blood; " it was as unchangeable as the " Laws of the Medes and Persians." In a court of justice Weeping Weasel saw a man arraigned who had wantonly slain a brother by sending a bullet through his heart. The crime had been seen by many; there was no conflicting evidence; it was premeditated; but again the counselors covered the case with doubt. The murderer had a bright, intelligent face and an undimmed intellect. Weeping Weasel heard him acquitted on the ground of temporary emotional insanity. The proceedings of that court were unfit for the uncivilized Kiowa.

Among the Kiowas, the position of medicine-man was one of great honor and trust, but extremely hazardous to the incumbent. When a warrior sickened the medicine-man was at once summoned. With rude rites, much beating of drums and strange incantations, he sought to drive away the disease. Sometimes he was unsuccessful and the patient died. When the corpse of his mismanagement was ready for burial the medicine-man was summoned, and he always came. He was divested of all his titles to respect, all the trophies he had gained by successful practice of physic, and manfully met his death on the scaffold with his victim.

Such was not the custom among the Pale-faces. Everywhere Weeping Weasel saw gilt-lettered signs of the medicine-man of the whites; yet the Pale-

faces died, and the same medicine-man ministered
to another. The savage also noticed that in this
strange country the physician never attended the
burial of his victim. Weeping Weasel concluded
that the death of the doctor had once been a
custom among the Pale-faces, but having fallen
into disuse the fraternity attended no funerals for
fear it might be revived.

Among the medicine-men of the Pale-faces,
Weeping Weasel found a class who with pictures
and posters attracted the eye to fabulous certifi-
cates of wonderful cures. They resided in great
houses wherein were all comforts, and where, with
endless noise and show, they professed to cure all
diseases by water, by physic, by pills, by powders,
by plasters, by new and strange remedies, even by
the laying on of hands. He found that while regular practitioners were allowed to live, these people
fared better even than they. They waxed fat and
grew rich upon the credulity of an ignorant public.
They lived and moved in the open glare of the
noonday sun. After all he had seen, Weeping
Weasel ceased to wonder at the strange epidemics
that sometimes prevailed among the Pale-faces.

He saw long trains, drawn by the mysterious
Pongo man, and managed by underpaid and care-

less workmen, collide with other trains, and as a result men and women were killed and children maimed ; yet no one was punished.

Our pilgrim now turned his face toward the capital of the great nation. One of the three horrible shapes shown him by Stone-Shirt must inevitably become his. But he did not look back. Civilization had caused him to think of the exhortations of the Pale-faced preacher. He " remembered Lot's wife."

The Massachusetts school teachers had displayed in rude letters on the walls of the lodge in which they taught this text from the scriptures: "The wicked flee when no man pursueth." In the city in which Weeping Weasel had just arrived he found that an officer of the Pale-face warriors was a defaulter to the sum of many thousands of the coins of his people. He was shamefully untrue! His position and name had been used to further defraud. There were no extenuating circumstances — there could be none. But the officer escaped, and no one followed and brought him back. Weeping Weasel was glad that he had burned the teachers at the stake, for he concluded they had willfully misrepresented the text hung upon the walls of the lodge, and that it should have read, " No man pursueth when the wicked flee."

In the Kiowa tribe all the councils were held
and the proceedings argued in a grave and digni-
fied manner. The pipe, signifying good will and
friendship, was first passed around. Each warrior
touched it with his lips. That day on the banks
of the Red River, when Weeping Weasel attempted
to tell me of the councils of the elders of the white
man, his breath was short, and much of what he
said was lost.

In that city he was told offices were bargained
for; the daughters of the Pale-faces solicited them
for their husbands and friends. He saw a cabinet
minister fall from his high place through the sale
of paltry positions.

Worn, harassed and broken in spirit, his pilgrimage useless, as no good could, in his opinion, come
to the savage from the white man's civilization,
Weeping Weasel turned his face towards the setting sun. He traveled as before, sleeping at night
under the stars, and again his drink came from
limpid streams; but his food was procured by a
revolver and magazine gun of the Pale-faces.
Civilization had taught him the deadly effect of
these weapons which he afterward used upon his
enemies and the Pale-faces themselves.

He returned to his tribe. His coming was seen

from afar. Without a word he entered his lodge :
he had no greeting for his faithful wives who
clustered around him.

Three days passed, and then Weeping Weasel
told to his people the story of his pilgrimage, told
what he had seen and heard, and the conclusions
he had drawn therefrom. With barbarous splendor he was tried for the crime of falsehood, which
is capital among Indians, all the men, women and
children of the tribe serving as judges.

In a great amphitheater of rock, at the junction
of the Pecos with the Rio Bravo del Norte, where
the swift rush and meeting of the two rivers forms
a whirlpool from which nothing can escape, the
public trials of the tribe were held, the people sitting for days in solemn judgment. If sentence of
death was decreed the body was thrown into this
fearful eddy, and watched by all the tribe as it
whirled, leaped, and sprang in the boiling water
until its final disappearance.

For generations and generations the gray and
frowning rocks had witnessed the trials of offenders
among the Kiowas. On one side rose sloping to
the bluff a half-circle of trees. So thickly grew
the branches of those pines and cedars that but
scant sunlight could filter through them. Custom

had decreed that if, at the moment of passing sentence, a ray of light should penetrate those thickly mingled branches and fall upon the face of the criminal, one-half of the sentence should be remitted.

The trial was as great as the occasion. Eagle Face, the oldest medicine-man of the tribe, was master of ceremonies. Flowing Hair, the favorite wife of Weeping Weasel, who had at one time, during five days of starvation, fed her first-born boy with blood drawn from her breast, was there, but silent, in her great fear, as became an Indian woman. Circumstances were against the pilgrim. Those wild savages could by no argument be brought to believe that there were such uncivilized people upon the face of the earth. If it were true, how could they live together? It was decided that sentence of death must be passed.

The chief, proud and defiant, took his stand against the half-circle of trees. Below, the pool was lashing itself into anger from a rising river. Flowing Hair had thrown herself at his feet as if to interpose her womanly strength against the dread sentence of an undeviating Indian code. At that moment a broad, imprisoned ray of light that had been entangled among the pines escaped and fell, in all its trembling warmth and pitying tenderness, upon the face of the wild Indian who had told the truth. In its soft caress it embraced the form of his fainting squaw.

Weeping Weasel escaped capital punishment, but was deposed from civil authority over the Kiowas, and was only obeyed as their supreme war-chief. His sentence further banished him, when stricken by death, from his tribe and from burial with his brethren. This was why I found him while dying, surrounded only by his family, on the banks of the Red River.

On the night of his death, to comfort a poor, dying soul, whose future seemed bright enough — although his religion was not mine — I told him, in the sign language, which his glazed and closing eyes could but dimly see, that, in my opinion, his tribe was nearer civilization than he dreamed, since to advanced ideas his sentence seemed just, and that he had only suffered the fate of all reformers.